NASCAR
OFF THE
RECORD

NASCAR OFF THE RECORD

BROCK YATES

MOTORBOOKS
INTERNATIONAL

First published in 2004 by MBI Publishing Company,
Galtier Plaza, Suite 200, 380 Jackson Street, St. Paul,
MN 55101-3885 USA

The information in this book is true and complete
to the best of our knowledge. All recommendations
are made without any guarantee on the part of
the author or Publisher, who also disclaim any liability
incurred in connection with the use of this data or
specific details.

We recognize that some words, model names and
designations, for example, mentioned herein are the
property of the trademark holder. We use them
for identification purposes only. This is not an official
publication.

MBI Publishing Company books are also available
at discounts in bulk quantity for industrial or
sales-promotional use. For details write to Special
Sales Manager at Motorbooks International
Wholesalers & Distributors, Galtier Plaza, Suite 200,
380 Jackson Street, St. Paul, MN 55101-3885 USA.

ISBN 0-7603-1726-7

Edited by Darwin Holmstrom
Designed by Rochelle Schultz

Printed in the United States of America

CONTENTS

Chapter One

WHISKEY TRIPPIN' BEGINNINGS

he France family didn't invent stock car racing any more than
James Watt and Thomas Edison invented electricity, but in both
cases they perfected and expanded the diverse commodities
into omnipresent elements of modern society. By the time William
Henry Getty France Sr. arrived in Daytona Beach in the spring of 1934
with his wife, Anne, and 1-year-old son, William Jr., his life was
committed to the booming world of automobiles and motorsports.

A native of backwater Horse Pasture, Virginia, 28-year-old
France had been raised in Washington, D.C., where, as a spindly 6-
foot, 5-inch high schooler, he had excelled in basketball. As a young
boy, his father had taken him to the incredible 1.125-mile, high-
banked—an amazing 48 degrees—board track at Laurel, Maryland,
where he had seen superstars like Ralph DePalma, Jimmy Murphy,
and Tommy Milton skate their Millers and Duesenbergs around the
wall-like corners at over 130 miles per hour. When his future as an
auto mechanic, part-time racer, and gas station operator seemed
bleak in the depression-ravaged capital district, he loaded up his
family and headed south.

Legend would have it that the was driving to Miami, but drew
up in Daytona Beach, 300 miles short of his goal, when his haggard
Hupmobile sedan broke down. France would later discount this as

nonsense, noting that as a mechanic, he could easily have repaired the old flivver and continued his journey. Daytona Beach was an obvious destination for a young motorhead, its vast expanse of breathtaking beach having been the scene of high-speed record attempts since the adventures of William Kissom Vanderbilt and Alexander Winton in the early years of the century. The beach had subsequently been the scene of countless assaults on the land speed record, including the tragic loss of Indy winner and self-taught design genius 26-year-old Frank Lockhart, when his tiny, bulletlike Stutz Blackhawk blew a tire at over 220 miles per hour on April 25, 1928. Later that same year, future Indy 500 winner Ray Keech set the LSR at 207.552 miles per hour with his ungainly four-ton White Triplex Special. In 1935, Sir Malcolm Campbell, aboard his Rolls-Royce aircraft engine-powered *Bluebird*, would run 276.82 miles per hour, the fastest speed ever recorded at Daytona Beach.

It was therefore understandable that Bill France would settle in this hotbed of high performance. He was an experienced race driver, having built and competed with several home-built single-seaters up north. While stock car racing existed, it still was a primitive, rural sport involving crude, backyard "jalopies" running on cow pastures in the outbacks of the nation.

There existed a thriving industry in high-performance parts for Ford engines, especially since Henry Ford's ultrahot flathead V-8 had hit the market in 1932. On the West Coast, the hot rod movement was running at full bore, with thousands of young men converging on the dry lakes at Muroc, Rosamond, El Mirage, and many others each weekend to run match races. In the South, Prohibition had only accelerated the region's tradition of distilling liquor without federal taxation, and bootlegging had become a major industry in the hard-wood forests of the Piedmont Plateau. The transportation of white lightning fell into the hands of expert drivers who began "whiskey trippin'," i.e., the high-speed hauling of the illegal booze from the hidden mountain stills to the major cities of the East Coast. With their rise came expert shade tree mechanics who, employing the speed equipment developed by West Coast hot rodders and their own ingeniousness, created blindingly fast coupes that could easily outrun the police and federal revenue agents' stock sedans.

By the 1930s, stock automobile racing had become a cheap and popular form of motorsport in most parts of the nation, but particularly on the Piedmont Plateau. There, the men who had honed their skills hauling liquor on the open roads began to run their modified Fords (called "Henrys"), Chevrolets ("Stovebolts"), Buicks ("Joe Lewises") and Lincolns ("Big Henrys") in patchwork races organized on crude, red-clay ovals carved out in small towns like Mt. Airy, Hickory, and Jonesville in North Carolina and Stockbridge in Georgia.

The races were ad hoc affairs, run on Sunday afternoons when liquor hauling was generally suspended in respect for the deep religious convictions of the rural South. No part of the nation had suffered more from the Depression. There being little industry besides the cotton mills, which paid a pittance for a week's hard labor, and with national demand for clothing at a nadir, the illegal liquor business offered a decent, if dangerous, living for daring young country boys. Bootlegging remained a viable business, even following the end of the Volstead Act, the 18th Amendment, and Prohibition in 1933.

A strange offshoot of the illegal liquor business was the creation of a class of expert drivers—daredevils who could navigate the backcountry roads of the Piedmont with amazing skill. Their favored vehicles were lightweight Ford coupes with hot-rodded V-8 engines—many built up by Atlanta engine genius Red Vogt—and stiffened rear springs to permit the transport of up to 180 gallons of white liquor, carried in either Mason jars or aluminum milk cans.

The best drivers could make five or six trips a week. At $40 a run, they made big money, which permitted them a Sunday rumble with their rivals on roughed-out ovals in the backcountry. Thirty or 40 of the trippers often lined up to do battle. There being no formal admission, the drivers passed their leather football helmets through the crowd, collecting nickels and dimes that would be added to the pot, sweetened by private bets between the competitors.

In 1936, having lost the land speed record seekers to the vast expanses of the Bonneville Salt Flats in Utah, the Daytona Beach business community organized a race for street stock automobiles on a 3.2-mile course that utilized the ocean front beach and a parallel, inland macadam highway.

The 240-mile race was won by Long Islander Milt Marion, driving, as expected, a modified Ford V-8 coupe. Bill France managed to finish fifth in a similar vehicle. The Daytona Beach course, with its luridly rutted corners, its ever-changing sandy beach surface, and its back-stretch barely wide enough for two cars, would remain a fixture of southern stock car racing until the Daytona International Speedway opened in 1959.

On November 12, 1938, a "national championship stock car race" was promoted at Atlanta's 1-mile Lakewood horse track. The 150-miler—which was shortened by darkness—was won by a scrawny 18-year-old named Lloyd Seay. Like most of the competitors, Seay was a whisky hauler, but he was a whisky hauler blessed with brilliant driving skills. Years later, Bill France Sr. would describe Seay as the "best pure race driver I ever saw." Seay would go on to win numerous stock car races, capped by victory at Daytona Beach in July 1941. But following another win on Labor Day, September 1, 1941, in the "championship" race at Lakewood, Seay's violent past in the world of bootlegging caught up with him. During an argument over a load of sugar, surely to be used in distilling white liquor, Seay was shot to death by his cousin, Woodrow Anderson, cutting short the life of stock car racing's first superstar.

By then Bill France had immersed himself in racing, both as a competitor and sometime promoter, while still operating his gas station in downtown Daytona Beach. At age 36 and with a family, France missed the draft when America entered World War II in December 1941; he remained in Daytona Beach for the duration, working on naval patrol boats. This would later cause Smokey Yunick—erratic NASCAR car builder, mechanical genius, archrival, and constant antagonist—to denounce him as a "draft dodger."

Yunick, a hard-edged mechanic from western Pennsylvania, had located in Daytona Beach following service in the war as a B-17 bomber pilot. In 1947 he had opened what he touted as "the Best Damn Garage in Town" and began applying his considerable skills to stock cars being campaigned by local stars Glenn "Fireball" Roberts and Marshall Teague.

Ironically, these four men—France, Yunick, Roberts, and Teague—would be primary figures in the foundation of postwar stock car racing and would create Daytona Beach as the epicenter of the new sport.

But if Daytona Beach was to become the capital of stock car racing following the formal organization of NASCAR (National Association of Stock Car Auto Racing) in 1947, the mother lode of talent and enthusiasm lay hundreds of miles to the north, in Charlotte, North Carolina. Within a 100-mile radius of the Queen City was a reservoir of great drivers and mechanics, all of which, like Seay, had honed their skills "whiskey trippin'." Among them were future greats like Curtis Turner; Junior Johnson; Herb Thomas; the Flock brothers, Fonty, Tim, and Bob; Lee Petty; Frank Mundy; and Cotton Owens. Others, like Elzie "Buck" Baker and Herb Thomas, came from working class backgrounds and drove city busses and

Two racing greats relax at Daytona prior to the 1963 500. Dan Gurney (left) had won the first of four consecutive Motor Trend 500s at Riverside a month earlier, while Glenn "Fireball" Roberts had just won the pole for the big race. Tragically, the popular and talented Roberts would succumb to burn injuries suffered at Charlotte on July 2, 1964. *Car and Driver archive*

Dan Gurney on his way to victory in the Motor Trend 500 at Riverside, California, January 1963. Gurney's brilliance as a driver coupled with his experience in Formula 1 and sports cars gave him a unique advantage over most of the NASCAR stars, whose racing experience involved oval tracks for the most part. *Car and Driver archive*

trucks for a living, but soon found new opportunities on the primitive ovals being bulldozed out of the loamy Piedmont soil.

The National Association for Stock Auto Racing—NASCAR— had been formed during a series of meetings at Daytona's beachfront, art deco Streamline Hotel in December 1947. In attendance with Bill France were Bill Tuthill, France's closest partner in the early days of NASCAR and holder of the title executive secretary; promoter Ed Otto; attorney Louis Ossinsky; businessmen Pat Purcell and Joe Epton; plus the organization's first commissioner, famed cross-country racer, motorcycle ace, and Indianapolis 500 veteran E.G. "Cannon Ball" Baker.

Other fledgling sanctioning bodies had been formed around the nation to take advantage of what appeared to be a boomlet in motor racing, but thanks to France's powerful personality, his earthy, Lincolnesque presence, and his brilliant business mind—which Yunick would later describe as "ruthless as Hitler"—it was not long before NASCAR rose to complete domination of the new sport.

NASCAR's first season in 1948 was a ragged patchwork of 52 races for the same modified coupes that had been perfected for bootlegging, driven in most cases by the same edgy young men who had learned their craft eluding the revenuers. It was not until 1949 that France created the elements of modern, big-league stock car racing with his "Strictly Stock Circuit" division—which became the "Grand National" in 1950. Rather than competing with prewar Ford coupes, the new series was designed for "1946 through 1949 American-made passenger cars available to the American public." Suddenly the door was opened to Detroit manufacturers, who were beginning to offer high-powered road cars to a performance-starved public. Leading the way were the new Cadillacs and Oldsmobiles, with their high-compression, pushrod V-8s.

While only eight Strictly Stock races were run in 1949, it was apparent that France and his associates had struck pay dirt. Not only were the manufacturers, now including Nash and Hudson, eager to demonstrate their new sedans in competition, but the crowds swarmed to the races, curious to see showroom-shiny automobiles banging fenders in 100-mile races. Some Detroit engineers opined that 100 miles around a lumpy, half-mile dirt track was equal to 50,000 miles of normal highway travel, and NASCAR began to tout its series as a "million-dollar proving ground."

The light, powerful Oldsmobile 88 in the hands of Atlanta professional Red Byron dominated the series, winning the championship. The 88s won five of the eight events that ranged up and down the East Coast from Daytona Beach in the south to the Erie County Fairgrounds 1,200 miles north in Hamburg, New York. (Lincoln won twice, and Plymouth won once.)

The following year, 1950, saw the Grand National series expand to 19 races with future superstars Curtis Turner, Fonty Flock, and 21 year-old Fireball Roberts in their 88s doing battle with the likes of Lee Petty and Johnny Mantz in their underpowered but nimble Plymouth coupes. It would be a Yankee, 22-year-old Bill Rexford of Conewango Valley, New York, who would be declared Grand National champion, thanks to his single victory at Canfield, Ohio, and other high finishes—he had 11 top-10 finishes in 17 starts. While tradition labels stock car racing as a pure southern sport, early years of Grand National competition saw almost half the races run north of the Mason-Dixon line. In 1950, 10 of the 19 Grand National 100-milers were run in front of Yankee crowds, with northerners like Rexford, Dick Linder, Jimmy Florian, Lloyd Moore, and Johnny Mantz winning 7 of the 19 races—including 3 by Pittsburgh's Linder in an Oldsmobile 88. While the roots of the sport were sprouting in the Carolinas and Florida, Grand National stock car racing was destined to bloom across the nation within the next four decades.

Life for the Grand National crowd was shockingly primitive, compared to the pomp and circumstance enjoyed by the drivers and teams of today. There were no palatial shops, massive 200-man staffs, expert mechanics and designers, Fortune 500 sponsors, endless hours of television and print media exposure, or sprawling superspeedways, where 200-mile per hour top speeds are now common.

The cars were stock sedans, slightly modified with stiffer springs, reinforced wheels, and rudimentary roll bars (not required and very seldom used until 1952). There were no massive 18-wheel transporters, or even trailers. The cars were generally flat-towed behind ragged sedans and station wagons, or even driven to the races. The tracks were generally half-mile and 1-mile ovals. A handful of tiny quarter-miler tracks, like that at Winston Salem's Bowman-Gray football stadium, were used for Modified, Sportsman, and NASCAR Short Track Division races.

France and his wife, Annie, ran the shows, trundling from track to track like vagabonds. "Big Bill" as he was now called, honchoed everything from prerace publicity to car inspections to overseeing the races. Annie handled the "back gate," the entry to the track's infield, taking payments in cash from the drivers, car owners, mechanics, local press, and the overtly curious.

It was in 1950 that the sport made its first great leap forward with the construction of the first superspeedway. South Carolina contractor Harold Brasington had ridden a bulldozer around a patch of farmland near the small city of Florence, thereby creating the legendary Darlington International Raceway—a 1.25, high-banked (26 degrees) rough oval that would demand monumental skill and bravery to negotiate. Brasington's ad hoc approach to track design resulted in a pear-shaped circuit with turns first and second narrower and oddly radiused. Brasington would later explain that he had to narrow up the first and second corners to avoid a minnow pond on the property.

The fast way around the new track produced a "Darlington Stripe," a scar of ruined body work on the right side of the car as drivers rode the steel guard rails through the fourth turn if maximum speed was to be gained. This fabulous old track, measured as 1.375 miles in 1953 and increased to 1.366 miles by new measuring methods in 1969, was to become a fixture in NASCAR racing—a veritable monument to stock car competition, once the Southern 500 was organized on Labor Day, 1950. (Actually, the first race at Darlington was officially named the "Southern Five-Hundred"—spelled out. In 1951, it became the "Southern 500.")

The race was almost not sanctioned by France. He feared that stock cars of the day might not last a full 500 miles of competition. But when the nascent Central States Racing Association offered to run the event, France decided at the last minute to participate. The CSRA and NACSAR cosanctioned the 1950 Southern 500, but the official souvenir program only had the CSRA logo on it—NASCAR was too late in joining the cosanction to get on the cover of the program. Playing to packed grandstands after 15 days of practice and qualifying, the race boomed away with Curtis Turner on the pole in his Oldsmobile 88.

While the lusty Olds, Lincoln, and Buick V-8s dominated the early stage of the race, tire wear proved to be the curse of the faster machines. Californian Johnny Mantz, driving his tiny Plymouth sedan powered by a wheezy, flat-head, in-line 6-cylinder, won the race by nine laps. He employed hard-compound truck tires to avoid the numerous pit stops encountered by his faster rivals. Ironically, his car was owned by a trio that included none other than Bill France.

Mantz was but one of 18 drivers out of the 75 car starting field to win any prize money. The rest of the competitors went home with their wallets empty, there being not enough cash to spread through the entire field, once all expenses were paid. Mantz and his three car owners won $10,835. By comparison, Johnnie Parsons, the winner of the 1950 Indianapolis 500 earlier that year, pocketed $57,458 for his rain-shorted drive to victory.

The creation of Darlington and the booming postwar economy combined to stimulate the NASCAR series perhaps quicker than either France or his codreamers in late 1947 had ever imagined. The horsepower race in Detroit was gathering steam, and by 1951 factory supported cars were being entered by GM's Oldsmobile and Buick Divisions, as well as by Chrysler, Studebaker, Nash, Ford, and Hudson—the last bringing to the tracks its new, low-slung Hornet sedans that featured "Twin H-Power"—dual carburetion. These machines, handled by experts like Herb Thomas and Marshall Teague, offered improved handling, thanks to their lower center of gravity, offsetting the power advantage enjoyed by rivals Fonty and Tim Flock and Curtis Turner with their "Rocket 88" V-8 Oldsmobiles.

A major turning point for France and his NASCAR tour came on August 12, 1951, during the running of the so-called "Motor City 250" at Detroit's 1-mile dirt oval on the Michigan State Fairgrounds. Just over 16,500 curious onlookers, including a number of key automobile industry executives, saw the NASCAR "good ol' boys" put on a fender-bashing, broadsliding, fence-busting display of mad-cap showmanship. The race devolved into a duel between Curtis Turner's Oldsmobile and young Tommy Thompson's big Hemi-powered V-8 Chrysler New Yorker. With 25 laps to go, as the pair hammered on each other through the rutted third turn, they collided, ripping open Turner's radiator. The legendary former bootlegger fought for control down the front straightaway as his engine exploded in a geyser of steam, giving Thompson a thrilling victory in the final laps.

The spectacle, which involved two high-marquee makes in a desperate struggle for victory, plus endless spins and crashes throughout the race, electrified Detroiters and their booming automobile industry. Many historians count this race as a seminal turning point in the history of NASCAR, in that it displayed, in all its noisy, violent glory, the potential for racing and selling production automobiles.

From that day on, domestic car manufacturers began to devote engineering and marketing efforts to winning races in France's spectacular "Grand National" series. Ironically, one of the contestants in the Detroit 250 field stood as an example of the immense rift that was beginning to tear at the fabric of American automobile racing. For most of the century, competition of all kinds had been controlled by the Contest Board of the American Automobile Association—an imperious pack of officials known as the "Chicago gang," who held an iron grip on the Indianapolis 500 and its satellite events. Bill France's NASCAR operated outside this empire, thereby being labeled as "outlaw" by the establishment.

Running a Cadillac coupe in the Detroit race was the 1949 Indianapolis 500 winner, Bill Holland, who had been banned by the AAA in 1950. Holland's expulsion came after running in a three-lap charity race in Opa Locka, Florida—an event unsanctioned by the AAA and therefore a mortal sin. Holland would be banished from the Indianapolis by 500 Chief Steward Harry McQuinn, an ex-driver himself. Bill France attempted to run his own open-wheel series with stock-block engines in 1952 and early 1953—both abbreviated seasons. McQuinn tossed France out of the Indianapolis Motor Speedway garage area during practice for the big race in 1954. Such overt power plays involving France and Holland only strengthened NASCAR, which was by the mid-1950s being viewed by the American motorsports establishment as a vibrant, potentially lucrative alternative to the rigid dictatorship of the AAA.

The American Automobile Association ended its involvement with racing in late 1955 following two tragedies, the death of Indianapolis 500 Champion Bill Vukovich while leading the 500 and the gruesome Pierre Levegh crash at LeMans that killed over 80 spectators. The United States Auto Club, a more liberal and accommodating coalition of car owners, track promoters, manufacturers, and drivers, replaced the AAA. Peaceful negotiations between NASCAR and USAC led to driver interchanges and other accords that permitted the two series to operate on generally parallel, noncompetitive tracks.

The USAC persisted with its own stock car racing series through the 1970s. But slowly, as the popularity of NASCAR racing spread across the nation, it became a harsh reality that no one, regardless of marketing savvy and financial backing, could compete with William H.G. France and his NASCAR organization when it came to running stock car racing, American-style.

France's development of the Daytona International Speedway in 1959 triggered a rash of new speedway construction in the South and forever set NASCAR on a steady upward course toward total domination of domestic motorsport.

American stock car racing was well on its way to becoming Big Business as the 1950s faded away, but the juicy images of hard-driving, whisky-trippin', good ol' boys bashing their way to glory formed the legendary foundations of the sport. While the Grand National series began to attract crowds outside the South, the elemental personality of stock car racing radiated outward from its rum-running, bootlegging origins. Its great drivers, Curtis Turner, Lee Petty, the Flock brothers, Buck Baker, Junior Johnson, et al, embodied this colorful Piedmont Plateau legacy and, despite efforts by public relations experts to excise that image, the men who had learned to race sliding through the hills and hollows of the Carolinas with a load of white lightning set forever the theme for this new and riveting form of racing that would slowly enrapture the entire nation.

Chapter Two

MY FIRST PEEK AT IMMORTALITY

I confess to being less than enthusiastic about stock cars when I was a young boy. In fact I hated them.

But my mother, a wonderfully multidimensional and enthusiastic lady, enjoyed automobile racing, and on warm summer nights often drove me twenty-five miles from our home in suburban Lockport, New York, 25 miles to Buffalo's Civic Stadium for the weekly midget races. The great bowl-shaped enclosure, now demolished, would later be the scene of the Buffalo Bills' early seasons and the setting of Robert Redford's wonderful baseball film, *The Natural*.

But in my childhood, the midget races dominated Civic Stadium. The powerful little cars were part of the wildly successful eastern tour that featured such superstars as Bill Schlinder, "Ted Tappett" (real name Phil Walters, who became the Number One driver for Briggs Cunningham's LeMans sports car team), George Rice, and other racing stars in their Kurtis-Kraft Offenhauser machines. They ran each Wednesday night on the paved quarter-mile, and I was mesmerized by the tiny, nimble, machines and their master drivers.

But the midget craze would not endure. The high cost of the Offy engines and the lack of competition led to a decline in the sport as the 1950s began. The midgets would be replaced at Civic Stadium by stock cars—not the slick, professionally run sedans competing on Bill France Sr.'s nascent NASCAR Grand National Circuit, but rather clapped out, beat-up Ford and Chevy coupes welded and bolted together in local garages and gas stations. They were ugly, unruly, sloppy machines; bog slow and prone to crashes and rollovers that seemed to amuse the huge crowds.

Eventually Ed Otto, the master promoter who organized the races at Civic Stadium and elsewhere along the East Coast, recognized that the slick, expensive, exotic midgets were a dying breed, and he replaced them with the local stockers. Otto was the cofounder of NASCAR, and he understood that feeder stock car races like those being run at Civic Stadium would only elevate interest in the Grand National series, and would therefore benefit the new form of auto racing that was beginning to sweep across the Southeast and trickle into the Northeast and Midwest.

My beloved Offy midgets were run off by a rag-tag mob of rumpled junkyard dogs that to me belonged in a crusher, not on a race track.

By the end of the 1950s, Grand National stock car racing had kicked into high gear. In 1959, Bill France Sr. had successfully financed the building of his Daytona International Speedway, a 2.5-mile, high-banked tri-oval that he hoped would become the world's fastest closed course. His dream suffered a setback in February, when Marshall Teague, the local veteran of both Grand National and Indianapolis 500 competition died in a crash at over 170 miles per hour—well short of the 176-mile per hour world's closed-course record set by Tony Bettenhausen in a Novi Indy car at Monza, Italy, the year before.

Indianapolis cars would not take kindly to Daytona. George Amick, another Indy car ace, was killed in April 1959 on the last lap of a USAC 100-miler. His death would mark the last time an open-wheel Indianapolis-type car would run at Daytona, even though brave little Amick had lapped the track at 176.887 miles per hour—a full 30 miles an hour faster than the fastest stock car speed, set by Bob Welborn at 143 miles per hour. Not only did France consider the Indy cars too fast for his track, but he was hardly interested in having the cars of a rival sanctioning organization out-perform his premier vehicles by such a wide margin.

Counterbalancing the disasters surrounding Indy cars during the first few weeks after the Daytona Speedway opened, the inaugural Daytona 500-miler on February 22, 1959, produced such a close finish that the winner was not determined until nearly three days following the end of the event. Three cars, driven by Johnny Beauchamp, defending Grand National Champion Lee Petty, and Joe Weatherly crossed the finish line virtually nose-to-nose. Weatherly was two laps behind and not a factor, but initial judgment by the officials gave the win to Beauchamp. But after 61 hours of nearly nonstop examination of all available film and still photos, the decision was reversed, and Petty was given the victory. This would help him to win the NASCAR championship in 1959, giving the former bootlegger his third title (1952, 1958, and 1959). Ironically his long and successful racing career would end on Daytona's fourth turn in 1961, when he and Beauchamp again tangled, this time sending both cars hurtling off the 31-degree Speedway corner. Both men suffered major injuries, but Petty's was by far the most critical.

Like all early NASCAR Grand National seasons, the drivers in 1959 faced a body-wrecking, 44-race schedule, often running twice a week across the Southeast with forays north of the Mason-Dixon line. Yet even with this grueling schedule, many of the drivers ran special events to enhance their incomes. While Petty was to take the title in 1959 after winning 11 times, he took home to his modest Randleman, North Carolina, frame house only $49,219 for his efforts. The same year Rodger Ward, the winner of the Indianapolis

The future "king" of stock car racing checks his Hemi engine in the Daytona garage area in February 1964. *Car and Driver archive*

The author watches Buck Sewell, Cotton Owens' mechanic, change a wheel bearing on David Pearson's Dodge Hemi at Bridgehampton, Long Island in 1964. *Car and Driver archive*

Richard Petty back in action at Daytona in 1968 following desperate efforts to repair a loose windshield. The solution was the lavish application of duct tape—known in the sport as "racer's tape." *Don Hunter*

500 was awarded $106,850 for only 3 1/2 hours behind the wheel. The 33rd finisher in the NASCAR point standings was Roy Tyner with 28 starts and seven top-5 finishes. Tyner won the grand total of $5,425. By contrast, Jimmy Bryan completed only one lap—at 31 miles per hour—of one of the 500s after nearly failing to start because of engine troubles and still made $3,405. Clearly, NASCAR had miles to go before parity would be reached with Indy-type racing in America.

In mid-September 1959 France had created a mad schedule involving a race at Richmond, Virginia, on September 13, then a week layoff for the teams to get to Sacramento, California, then back to Hillsboro, North Carolina, for a night race on September 20. Many eastern teams, including that of the Petty operations, chose not to make the western haul.

This afforded Ed Otto, the canny promoter whose racing roots lay in the Northeast, to arrange a special appearance for the Pettys in a so-called "stock car versus sports car" challenge he helped organize at the Harewood road course in Jarvis, Ontario, on the flatlands northwest of Toronto. Otto, a New Jersey native, had been promoting motorcycle and automobile racing since 1927. He joined with the Canadian Race Drivers Association to stage the race, stirring the pot in veteran promoter fashion in July, when he told the Canadian press, "A late-model U.S. production stock car could beat a sports car on any track over any distance." This statement, made during a time when the rivalry between "sporty cars" and "Detroit iron" was at its peak, elicited outrage among the imported car loyalists, and a major effort was undertaken to bring a strong field of sports cars to the 100-mile race.

The Harewood road course was a 1.9-mile flat, rough triangle that had opened 10 years earlier, following the abandonment of the property by the Royal Canadian Air Force. It was one of dozens of airports in the United States and Canada being utilized as temporary roadracing circuits.

Ed Otto was vice president of NASCAR and a key player in that growing organization. He had promoted a number of races in Canada, including the first ever for all-time superstar Richard Petty. It was 1 year earlier that the 21-year-old had taken the wheel for the first time on the quarter-mile oval at the Canadian National Exposition Grounds in Toronto—where his father punted him into the fence on his way to victory. Richard had also run in the first Daytona 500 earlier in the year, driving an Oldsmobile convertible and would be declared Rookie of the Year at the end of the season.

Otto arranged for both Pettys, father and son, to enter their Plymouth Belvedere stock cars, Nos. 42 and 43, for the Harewood event. He also persuaded seven other area drivers from western New York, Ohio, and Ontario to bring their Chevrolets and Fords to face the "sporty cars."

On the other side was a formidable contingent led by the great John Fitch, the former Mercedes-Benz team driver who, while winding down his career, remained one of the fastest roadracing drivers in North America when at the wheel of his Cooper-Monaco. Also entered were young star Harry Blanchard in a potent Porsche RSK and Canadian Harry Entwhistle in a light, powerful Lotus 15. Not only did the sports car drivers outnumber their stock car rivals, but their cars—light and powerful and fitted with massive brakes—were radically better suited for roadracing than the 3,700-pound NASCAR stockers, regardless of Otto's boasting.

It was during this period that professional sports car racing was on the rise, after having been locked in an English-style, purely amateur pose for decades. John Fitch was a leader in the professional movement and a month earlier had staged a similar race at his Lime Rock Park track in northwestern Connecticut. There Indy winner Rodger Ward had bested a powerful field of sports cars, not in a NASCAR stocker, but rather in one of my beloved

Offenhauser midgets. This race electrified the racing community and energized interest in the so-called "International Challenge" being staged at Harewood.

Being a young, eager enthusiast, I climbed into my new Triumph TR-3 sports car and headed north to Harewood to witness the anticipated shootout.

The day was cool, with a brisk breeze off nearby Georgian Bay whistling through the masses of cars jamming the concrete paddock. A crowd of over 10,000—claimed at the time to be the largest ever for a motor race in Canada, lined the fences. I had seen a number of the sports cars compete at Watkins Glen, so my curiosity was centered on the Pettys. Due to a Grand National race set for the following night in Hillsboro, North Carolina, the Pettys had brought only one car—father Lee's Number 42 Plymouth—while Richard's Number 43 (listed in the program as "Dick" Petty—a nickname he despised) stayed in the South.

Lee Petty had come north for a few hundred dollars in "deal" or "appearance" money to add marquee value to the show. With a modest purse and massive miles to travel, Otto had paid the great driver to show up, drive a few laps and leave. Such are the backdoor deals involving celebrity appearances of top-flight race drivers in minor events that exist to this day.

As expected, the race was a blowout for the sports cars. Blanchard won after Fitch's fuel-line broke eight laps from the end. Only five stock cars appeared, and two were running—dead last—at the end. Lee Petty ran three laps and retired with what the *Toronto Globe and Mail*—a major sponsor of the race—described as "fuel pump trouble."

As the race wound down, I went to the Petty "pit" in the infield—no more than a patch of grass where their Plymouth (no doubt in perfect shape) sat behind a large Oldsmobile 98 sedan. With no trailer or transporter for the Plymouth, it had been flat-towed to the race behind the Oldsmobile, looking more like a used car on the way to an auction than a first-class NASCAR machine.

I stood in amazement as Petty's two sons, Richard and his younger brother, Maurice, jacked up the Plymouth and scrambled underneath to remove the drive shaft. Once it was clear, they stuffed it into the gaping trunk of the Olds and hooked a tow-bar to the front bumper of the Plymouth.

Their rig ready to roll south, the boys hauled a small grille out of the Oldsmobile's back seat and a bag of charcoal. Once the fire was lit, Lee Petty opened a can of Campbell's Boston Pork and Baked Beans and sat it on the grille to warm. Dinner was served.

The legendary Petty family, who would, as drivers and car owners, win nearly 500 NASCAR races, sat around the little campfire and ate their supper. No giant Newell motor coaches, no 18-wheel Kenworth transporters, no hovering public relations agents, no legions of uniformed crewmen, no executive jets, no first-class hotel suites; just pork and beans on an open fire in a grassy paddock in a vacant corner of Canada.

Who could imagine the glory days that lay ahead, not only for the Petty family, but for the entire world of NASCAR stock car racing?

Chapter Three

A TOUGH TOUR WITH COTTON'S STOCK CARS

S hortly after I came to work for *Car and Driver* at its Park
Avenue offices in Manhattan in the spring of 1964, I became
good friends with B.F. "Moon" Mullins, the Dodge public relations representative for the East Coast. A gregarious Irishman with
a background in newspaper work, Mullins was widely liked and
respected in the New York automotive community. He was a
straight-shooter, devoid of the gooey corporate slickness that often
personified men in his profession.

In those days NASCAR Grand National drivers (as they were
known before Winston cigarettes assumed the title sponsorship of
their series) made a so-called Northern Tour each summer. On the
schedule were five or six races up and down the East Coast, ranging
from short track events at Old Bridge, New Jersey and Islip, on
Long Island, to road courses at Bridgehampton, also on Long Island,
and Watkins Glen in the Finger Lakes district of upstate New York.
Earlier that year, Chrysler Corporation had unveiled its incredible
426-ci Hemi, a monstrous, short-stroke V-8 featuring hemispherical
combustion chambers similar to those offered on high-performance
Chryslers, Dodges, and DeSotos 10 years earlier. In February 1964,

young Richard Petty had scored his first superspeedway victory in the Daytona 500. His Number 43 Petty-blue Plymouth Hemi had led all but 16 of the 200 laps. Two other Hemi-powered cars had finished second and third. While protests rumbled from the Ford, Mercury, Pontiac, and Chevrolet headquarters in Detroit that the Hemi engines were nonproduction and therefore ineligible for NASCAR competition, boss Bill France decided to let them compete, with the proviso that versions of the engine would soon to be offered to the public. Hemi-powered Plymouth Barracudas and Belvederes and Dodge Challengers and Coronets would ultimately be produced for road use, but not until after NASCAR had banned the engines in 1965, following threats of boycott from the other Detroit manufacturers. This in turn had prompted Chrysler to quit NASCAR for that season in protest. But during the remainder of competition during the 1964 season, there was little that could touch the Hemis in terms of raw power. Petty won 9 of the 61 NASCAR races he competed in (62 were run) and wrapped up the first of his seven championships. Consistent driving by Ford driver Ned Jarrett and Mercury star Bill Wade kept those two marques in contention.

Leading the Dodge contingent were veteran Spartanburg race driver, mechanic, and car owner Everett "Cotton" Owens and his hometown driver, David Pearson—a hard-driving, slow-talking good ol' boy, who is remembered as one of the most versatile stock car drivers of all time. It was then the policy of the Dodge management in Detroit that no matter the outcome of the race, Pearson's white and red Number 6 Dodge Coronet Hemi would at all cost start on the pole or up front and contend for the lead while running. Being a natural charger, this style of driving suited Pearson perfectly. He and Owens, both fiercely competitive behind their soft-spoken Carolina demeanors, came to every race prepared for a kamikaze-style assault for all-out victory. Second place was nowhere to this pair.

As the NASCAR teams headed north in July 1964 a pall hung over the sport. In January, popular "Little Joe" Weatherly had crashed at Riverside Raceway's Turn 6 and died on January 19, 1964. On May 24, Glenn "Fireball" Roberts had been involved in a horrific crash at the Charlotte Motor Speedway and suffered massive burns when his Ford's fuel tank—unprotected by fuel cells that had yet to be developed—ruptured. Roberts, one of the best-liked drivers on the tour, fought for his life until he succumbed on July 2, just prior to the tour leaving for Yankee country.

In those days, stock car drivers drove in their street clothes, protected only by a helmet and seat belt. No fireproof coveralls, no shoulder harnesses, no gloves, no goggles. Little more protection than the average motorists driving to work.

David E. Davis Jr., editor of *Car and Driver*, and I worked out a plan with Mullins whereby I would travel with the Owens/Pearson team from July 10 to July 19, while they raced at Bridgehampton, Islip, and Watkins Glen, eating and sleeping with the team and even helping in pit stops. I was to meet their big Dodge flatbed hauler on the New Jersey turnpike following their race at Old Bridge, then to carry on north to Bridgehampton for the first major roadrace of the tour.

NASCAR staged races on road courses at California's Riverside Raceway, at Bridgehampton, and at Watkins Glen. These events required substantially different suspension and chassis setups than for the oval tracks on which the cars normally ran. While some drivers, like Pearson, enjoyed roadracing, many of the NASCAR regulars felt uncomfortable navigating left- and right-hand turns, and the varying radius corners of the road courses. Some held "sporty car" drivers in disdain, feeling they lacked the cojones for the hard-edged, fender-banging combat required in oval racing.

This attitude would best be exemplified at Bridgehampton by tough Carolinian driver Neil "Soapy" Castles, a quintessential redneck. When Castles arrived at Bridgehampton, he sauntered up the office where a group of young women representing the Sports car Club of America were handling registration. On that weekend the NASCAR drivers would run the feature race on Sunday while amateur sports cars drivers raced on Saturday.

Castles, lighting a Camel from a pack he kept rolled up in his T-shirt sleeve, asked one of the secretaries, "We all gonna be able to race against them sport car boys?"

"No, Mr. Castles, they're racing on Saturday. You'll compete on Sunday." Said one of the young girls.

"Aw, shit." Said Castles taking a deep drag on his Camel, " Was fixin' to kill me a couple of them little gentlemen."

Such was the world I entered with Cotton Owens and David Pearson on that warm summer night in 1964.

The Ride Begings.

"Wade never shoulda won that race. You can't go 100 miles on a 22-gallon tank. It just can't be done," complained Bud Allman as he squinted against the oncoming lights of the New Jersey Turnpike traffic.

Buck Sewell, stretched across the rear seat of the four-place cab on the big Dodge truck in a state of utter exhaustion, mumbled his agreement, but a third rider noted that the protest lodged by Billy Wade's archrival, Ned Jarrett, had been disallowed and Wade's first NASCAR Grand National stock car race victory at Old Bridge, N.J., was now official.

"I ain't saying ol' Billy didn't run good. His Mercury was really handlin', and on a flat half-mile that's real important. But you can't go 100 miles on no 22 gallons of gas," Allman repeated. Their driver, David Pearson, who at that moment trailed them through the night, had commanded the race for much of the distance until a stop to change a soft tire put him out of contention.

"That's the second race in a row that we've lost by a fluke," said Allman. He was built like a middleweight, with powerful shoulders set on a chunky, compact body. His face was furrowed in the harsh glare of the headlights and only the absence of scar tissue around his eyes indicated that his life had not been spent in sweaty gyms and prize rings.

"But your luck is gonna change at Bridgehampton. Ain't that right, Buck?"

Sewell had managed to find a position of relative comfort amidst the litter of magazines, spare parts, shoes, and road maps and was now in a deep sleep. "Lookit that SOB. When we get to the motel, he'll swear he never slept a wink. You wait."

The little caravan threaded its way through the labyrinth of streets and parkways between the George Washington Bridge and the Long Island Expressway. Allman was an uncertain leader with the flatbed truck that carried the red and white Number 6 Dodge stock car that had run at Old Bridge. Behind him came Pearson, the only man awake in the Dodge Station wagon that also carried the boss, Cotton Owens, and his wife and son. Bringing up the rear—until they became separated exiting the bridge—was the second truck, driven by mechanic Dean Turner, towing the second red and white Number 6 Dodge stock car, an identical vehicle except that it was set up to run in the two roadraces scheduled on NASCAR's annual tour of the North.

A thousand miles, three races, and no victories lay between them and the familiar red clay of Spartanburg, South Carolina. Four more Grand Nationals would have to be run in the alien Yankee surroundings before they would return.

"This week is gonna be a bitch," said Allman firmly. "We gotta get one car ready for Bridgehampton, then change the transmission on the car we ran tonight at Old Bridge. Just won't go into first gear. Yep, it's gonna be a bitch."

It was 4:30 Saturday morning when the Cotton Owens racing team—minus one truck and one stock car—arrived at a fog-shrouded motel outside Riverhead, Long Island.

"Boy, sure wish I'd got me some sleep on the way," grumped Buck as he staggered toward his room.

"See that?" growled Bud. "Ain't that something."

The bedside telephone rattled them awake at 8:30 and, after a long interlude of cursing and eye rubbing, Allman, Sewell, and Pearson climbed into the truck to drive the remaining 30 miles to Bridgehampton.

Dressed in the short-sleeved sport shirt that was the trademark of the NASCAR stock car drivers, David Pearson drove the truck as fast as it would go, taking obvious delight in hearing the engine roar its protest against downshifts through the two-speed rear axle, while honking and waving at every bystander along the route. He looked younger than his 30 years and his fresh, tanned face bore no scars after nearly 10 years of violent racing in the southern stock car circuit.

Dean Turner and Dave Parsons, a youthful assistant mechanic, showed up in the paddock area looking bleary-eyed after snatching a few fitful hours of sleep in the cab of their truck. Nonetheless, they had already unloaded the Dodge and were in the process of fitting it with fresh tires when the rest of the crew arrived.

Set on a bleak hump of sand in the middle of the track, the Bridgehampton pit and paddock area was pervaded by an air of eternal desolation, despite the double clutter of the stock cars and a small field of sports cars that were running a regional race in conjunction with the NASCAR event. Hunkered down beside the wall of a hot dog stand to seek shelter from a powerful midmorning sun,

Pearson surveyed the landscape and was moved to comment, "This here's the end of the earth, and that ain't no crap."

Other teams began to arrive, the larger ones like the Pettys, Bud Moore, and Ned Jarrett bringing at least two identical cars, while others hauled in older, more battered machines with aged trucks and tired station wagon tow cars.

Practice started in the late morning, and a row of bellowing stock cars had moved to the starting line before David Pearson walked over to the van and dug a battered Bell helmet from a side tool compartment. He donned it—his only concession to modern safety measures—and got into the car through the window. Someone asked Allman why Pearson didn't wear fireproof coveralls and a shoulder harness. "Hell, he's run without a helmet less'n they stopped him," Allman replied. "But he does wear coveralls in the big races."

They thundered down the pit lane and appeared moments later in a massive, organic formation of bright colors and deafening noise. The green flag fell and the furious dicing began. The drivers seemed to forget that this was a practice session. The SCCA corner observers were thrown into panic as they witnessed the entire field swoop off the corners and onto Bridgehampton's treacherous, sandy shoulders. The course marshal's switchboard was flooded with distraught voices reporting every car leaving the course at every corner . . . until it was discovered that NASCAR stock car drivers took a more casual approach to line with 3,700-pound stock cars than did their roadracing counterparts.

Pearson interrupted his part in the fun to arrive at the pits and report that the car was geared too low and the suspension was too stiff. Sewell and Parsons silently wheeled a jack into position at the rear of the car and began work. A 4:30 rear end was installed in 15 minutes, while Allman and Dean removed two leaves from each rear spring.

Petty, who had been going very rapidly, swung by at the end of the practice session to find out what was ailing the Dodge. "I followed Pearson awhile, figuring that he could show me the right line. Then when I knew he didn't know where he was going either, I passed him." Allman and the boys dissolved into laughter while Pearson looked sheepish and puffed on his cigarette.

"I'm gonna git me some potted meat," Buck announced, and the entire crew—including Cotton Owens, who had arrived shortly before noon looking considerably refreshed—trooped off to the big truck where they lunched on potted meat and Pepsi-Cola. All the while, practicing sports car buzzed in the background.

A brief 10-lap qualifying heat ended practice. Pearson pushed Richard Petty hard for a few laps, then fell back to finish second. He reported that the new rear end was a big improvement, though it meant having to navigate the entire back sector of the circuit with the Dodge bellowing at 7,000 rpm in third gear.

On the way back to the motel, Pearson raced Ned Jarrett's van along the winding road that led away from the race track. He finally captured the lead, accelerating by as the two trucks exited a blind curve, and swept away with a final blast on the horn. Lighting a plastic-tipped cigar, Allman surveyed the sandy Long Island land-scape dotted with scrub pines. "This looks kinda like home," he observed wistfully, "with them pines and all."

"Maybe, but I'd rather be home in jail than up here," said Pearson.

Later at the motel where we were staying, showered and stoked with well-done sirloin, the crew received an invitation from the motel owner to attend the weekly Saturday evening floor show and party that he ran in the recreation room. They arrived looking all buffed and polished and took a table near the bank, while a retired dress salesman told some jokes and a local girl struggled through a selection of pop tunes. The evening dragged on, and most

David Pearson and the author appear concerned about their prospects prior to the Bridgehampton race. Pearson drove No. 6 throughout his long career with the Cotton Owens team. *Car and Driver archive*

Not exactly a top-flight NASCAR pit crew. The author hauls away a used tire during a Bridgehampton pit stop as Buck Sewell confers with Pearson. *Car and Driver archive*

Buck Sewell, David Pearson (back to the camera), and the author confer prior to the start of the night race on Islip, Long Island's 1/5-mile, saucer-sized oval. Pearson drove in the same pants and short-sleeved shirt, wearing only a helmet and goggles for rudimentary protection. *Car and Driver archive*

of the guests, including Owens and his wife, went off to bed. Dean and Parsons hung on as long as possible then gave in to the memory of two sleepless nights and disappeared. Shortly after midnight, a busload of southern newspapermen and their wives arrived as guests of Dodge, and the sagging festivities picked up tempo. A card game started on the ping-pong table, and Pearson, now decked out in a lei, chatted vociferously with everyone.

Referred to by some of the press as "Li'l Abner," Pearson appears on the surface to be a simple country boy with a sort of empty-headed good humor and little or no concern for anything but driving fast. His exterior hides no significant complexities, but he is far from an affable oaf. Like many southern stock car drivers, Pearson grew to prominence in a highly provincial sport, cheered by a small pocket of fans with whom he had a great rapport.

Today, with NASCAR stock car racing a giant business under the close scrutiny of major automakers and oil and tire companies, Pearson and his friends find themselves national figures, with resultant demands for witty press statements and cogent remarks to the television cameras. They resemble the country music stars who make the big time and find the harsh exposure of New York show business terribly brutal, in contrast to the amateur atmosphere of Nashville.

"I hate to make speeches. That's the one thing about this business that bothers me," Pearson recently confessed. "They wanted me to do a radio show in Spartanburg about stock cars. I tried it for a few nights and felt like a damn fool. Hell, all them people listening in knew me, so what did they want to hear me talkin' on the radio for anyway?"

Allman and the crew were up early Sunday and on the way to the track without Pearson or the Owens family, who were sleeping late. Conversation centered on the possible resumption of the Wade-Jarrett feud that had begun a few weeks before when they began bumping each other in a 100-miler. Wade won a doubtful first-round victory when he roared out of the pits, met Jarrett as he entered the first turn, and slammed him into the fence. But Bud Allman was speaking the opinion of the majority when he said, "Ol' Ned is waitin' his time, and he'll git him, you wait." Having been Jarrett's chief mechanic for five years before joining the Owens team, Allman's statement carried the ring of authority.

The paddock was beginning to fill by the time they arrived and unloaded the car. Darel Dieringer, a square-jawed Hoosier who was one of the few northerners to run the circuit, wandered over as Allman was changing plugs. A teammate of Wade's, he generally restricted his efforts to the major NASCAR speedway and roadraces.

"You sure were a brave mother, runnin' that close behind Paul Goldsmith like you done in practice," said Allman.

"Hell, I had to keep up," said Dieringer, a broad smile crossing his face.

"You know he was outta control over all them back corners?"

"Hell, yes."

"How would you know? You was too close to him to see."

"What do you mean too close? I could see him wavin' at me with his elbows. Man did he take a ride."

Allman laughed. "Was it a good 'un?"

"Man, oh man, way over yonder. He musta gone 100 yards off the track."

Because they are so well protected in the massive roll cages and bodywork, NASCAR drivers take great delight in recounting the wild exit of a competitor from the track. So long as no personal injury is involved, a spin or crash is a great source of amusement, and anyone being so indiscreet as to lose control in spectacular fashion can count on being ribbed mightily.

As race time approached, sports car types milled curiously around the stock cars, seemingly oblivious to the one-hour regional event that was droning monotonously onward out on the track. The NASCAR boys, unused to rubbing elbows with the female gender in pit and paddock areas, went about their work with erotic fantasies dancing through their heads. The display of tight slacks and shorts left them breathless with excitement. "I'm gonna git me a sporty car and some tennis shoes an' see if Ah cain't pick me up one of them frazzly haired dollies," drawled one as he slid beneath a car.

That day's Grand National race was an exquisite punishment of the senses. The stock cars engaged in a desperate battle over the entire 150-mile distance. Richard Petty lunged off the pole position (from a flying start) and led half a lap, until he spun. Pearson, Dieringer, Goldsmith, and Wade then grappled for first, while Petty raced after them. He had regained all but eight seconds when he rolled into the pits with a blown engine. Goldsmith fell by the wayside, then Dieringer, leaving Wade and Pearson to fight it out. Though the Dodge had probably 10 more horsepower, Wade was able to hang on by dint of better handling, and the two exchanged the lead on several occasions.

"Pearson's runnin' hot," shouted Allman as he roared past the pits with Wade snubbed against his rear bumper. The crew agreed that they had seen their driver pinch his nose—that standard signal for high temperatures—though he later explained that he was "just waving' at ol' Billy."

As serious as a driver as Pearson is, the Bridgehampton race did not bring him to a competitive peak. Like some of his fellows, he thoroughly enjoyed the road course and went about his work with considerably more jocularity than might be expected from a hardened professional. Following the race, Wade reported that during the peak of his dice with Pearson, he had spun wildly.

"When I was flyin' off yonder, I looked over and there was ol' Pearson smilin' at me. You know, that son-of-a-gun slowed down and waited for me?"

Pearson and Wade each made a frantic pit stop and their crews tossed aboard 22 gallons of fuel in 20 seconds. Tire changes weren't necessary. With 11 laps remaining, the lead seemed to be opening in favor of Pearson and the Owens crew was sensing victory. Then their man coasted into the pits. His engine had blown.

Pearson climbed somberly out of the car, his navy blue sports shirt bathed in sweat, and lit a cigarette. The curious swept around him while he and Owens discussed the ailment. There was nothing to do but load the car and go home. Wade went on to win his second consecutive Grand National race, with Buck Baker a distant second (Baker was 20 seconds behind Wade at the finish).

Monday was gripped in a gray summer rain when Owens and the rest left Riverhead for the 50-mile trip to Islip, Long Island, where a 300-lap race was scheduled for the one-fifth mile Islip Speedway on Wednesday night. Owens discussed his plans as he headed through the miserable weather. "We'll replace the transmission in the short track car at the motel tomorrow. Then, after Islip, we'll pull the engine and use it as a spare for the car that we run at Watkins Glen in Sunday. Dean and Parsons can take the short track car home and start helpin' the other fellers get ready for Bristol." (At that very moment, several other mechanics were laboring in Spartanburg to prepare two Dodges for the Volunteer 500 at Bristol, Tennessee. Pearson and newcomer Earl Balmer would drive.) "Then me, Buck, and Bud will change the blown engine at the Glen. I don't like to split the crew up this way, but when you're this far from home, you ain't got much choice."

The next two days, which continued cold and rainy, were spent in the parking lot of a motel near Islip changing the transmission and making routing preparations for the 300-lapper. Several other crews, including Bud Moore's, Lee Petty's, and Ray Fox's, were working in the same lot, and the drudgery was relieved by sporadic crap games for rather impressive amounts of money. Wednesday dawned sunny, and the morning was spent horse-playing at the motel's pool prior to the race that evening.

Compared to most of the tracks on which the Grand National stock cars run, Islip was a silly miniature; compared to Bridge-hampton it was like running on the rim of a china saucer. One-fifth of a mile of slightly banked pavement, rimmed with rickety grand-stands, it was the scene of weekly races for assorted outlaw modified stock cars, occasional midget events, and Figure-8 races, which were televised on ABC's *Wide World of Sports*. The Grand National cars looked outlandishly large as they skidded and wor-ried their way around the tiny oval during practice. But their bulk was deceiving, and after a short time Wade, Pearson, Petty, and Jarrett were lapping at 14 seconds.

Wade's good fortune continued, and by the time trials ended he had secured the pole position in his faithful black and red Mer-cury. He was smaller than most of the drivers, probably not more than 150 pounds, and, like Pearson, looked younger than his 34 years. A shy native of Houston, Texas, who had raced in the dusty backwaters of the sport for a decade before getting his break with the Cotton Owens team the year before, Wade's two consecutive wins had been absolutely unexpected—probably even to himself. He bantered with his fellow drivers with noticeable self-consciousness, as if he feared that any display of satisfaction over his recent glories would somehow jinx his luck. Whatever Wade was doing, he was doing it right. He would not err for two more races.

Pearson managed to qualify fourth, though he complained that the car was not handling and was down on power. The sun had disappeared and the meager battery of lights had been turned on around the track when Cotton Owens gathered his crew together in the paddock, "We ain't takin' no rubber to the pits," he said firmly, "just some gas."

"But Cotton," protested Buck Sewell, "if Pearson cuts a tire or something, we gonna have to change . . ."

"We ain't gonna change no tires, Buck, and that's that. On a lousy little track like this, a stop for rubber will cost you a minimum of five laps. If you're leadin', you'll lose at least five places and it stands to reason you'll be lucky to finish higher than fifth or sixth. For the purse they're payin', it ain't worth the wear and tear on the car. It just ain't economical, and that's all there's to it." Coming from Owens, a man who had begun racing in the woolly days following the war and became one of the greatest drivers in the business before eye trouble forced him to retire, the strategy made sense.

The race started with 22 of the big automobiles wedged onto the tiny track. The insiders knew the traffic would clear slightly during the early stages, as it had at Old Bridge, because Lee Petty would cruise awhile and come in with his son's spare. Jarrett's mechanic, James Henry, would do likewise with their extra car, and Darel Dieringer was planning to save his Mercury for Watkins Glen after a few casual laps.

Somehow the field swept through the opening stages without incident, and Wade jumped into a short lead. The noise filled the arena until it hammered all attempts at speech into particles of nonsense and the crews resorted to communication with a series of impromptu hand signals. The cars swirled around until the leader mingled completely with the stragglers and there was no discernable beginning or end to the field. The faster cars used the outside groove for passing, and it was while Bob Welborn was putting a lap on a slower car that he lost control and whacked the wall. Wade nicked him during the flurry and rushed into the pits to have his crew bend the left fender away from the tire with a crowbar. Pearson, who was holding fourth while understeering badly in corners, came in for fuel. But it was all for naught. A few laps after the caution flag had been lifted, he nudged a car, and the dented bodywork cut apart the left rear tire. Pearson limped into the infield and parked.

Shortly after the halfway point, Wade was closing in to lap the second-place car, driven by Ned Jarrett, and attention in the pits centered on the expected confirmation. A knowing smile crossed Allman's face as he pointed to the two cars. The track was so small that the crewmen in the middle were forced to spin in a small circle to keep up with Wade and Jarrett—as if they were tethering gas-powered model airplanes in flight.

Wade caught his rival as they accelerated onto the short back-stretch and whipped to the outside. Jarrett countered by steering hard right, forcing the Mercury into the wall. Had he waited a split second longer, he would have had his man, but, in an error caused by eager-ness, he moved too early and Wade escaped by slamming on the brakes. Now it was Wade's turn. It is within the repertoire of every major-league stock car driver to spin an adversary by nosing inside during the entry to a corner and shoving him out of the way, but this tactic is generally so neatly executed that no one can honestly say that it was not an accident. But if Wade could have picked off Jarrett it would have been no accident. Several times the substantial front bumper of the Mercury hooked into the blue flank of the Ford, but Jarrett wriggled free. He was driving as fast as he could, aware that a slackening of pace would bring Wade against him like a freight train. At the same time Wade was trying to figure a way to nip past Jarrett without leaving himself vulnerable. The duel continued unresolved for several laps until, with what seemed to be an undeclared truce, Jarrett suddenly moved to the outside and Wade rushed past.

After he had taken the checkered flag for his third race in a row, Wade burst out of his car and was about to strike out after Jarrett on foot when his crew members grabbed him. Though not moved to violence against a man whom he outweighed by 40 pounds, Jarrett kept the feud alive by again protesting Wade's victory, claiming the scorers had missed a lap when Billy stopped for repairs.

On Thursday, two days before the 150-miler at Watkins Glen, Sewell and Allman drove to the track's technical inspection building, where they teamed with Owens to change engines in the Dodge and prepare it for Saturday's race. Dean and Parsons left for home with the other truck, and the Dodge public relations people arranged for Pearson to remain on Long Island to run a drag race against Richard Petty on Friday evening.

There was precious little joking at Watkins Glen. The Cotton Owens team needed to win badly to buoy their spirits. Pearson stood a solid fourth in the point championship, with four Grand National victories to his credit for the season, but the recent famine was beginning to blur those memories. Three of the last four races had been in Pearson's pocket when mechanical trouble slowed him, and that bothered Owens, Sewell, and Allman terribly. A thunderstorm was rattling against the sheet metal building as Cotton tightened the last bolt on the replacement engine's water pump and looked up, unsmiling, at Allman. "Pearson ain't gonna drive this race track like he did at Bridgehampton. He does, an' he's gonna find himself planted against a tree."

Everyone, including Pearson, was careful on Saturday. They drove with every intention of staying within the Glen's unforgiving perimeters, and therefore lap times were not quite as impressive as on the Long Island circuit (where Petty had gotten to within fours seconds of the absolute track record.)

Still unhappy with the handling, Pearson managed to qualify fifth. Wade was on the pole beside his old acquaintance, Ned Jarrett, as the field streamed across the starting line and squirmed out of sight over the hill. Thundering up the straightaway, LeeRoy

Yarbrough's Dodge dug a couple of wheels into the shoulder and flung a stone against Pearson's windshield. It smashed into the cockpit like a machine gun slug, spraying glass into his right eye. Half blinded, he struggled on through the July heat. His depth perception gone, he drove too deep into several corners and spun trying to maintain his position. By the halfway point the pain had become unbearable, and Pearson rapped his helmet as he accelerated past his pits. "He wants relief," shouted Owens, and Sewell raced off in search of Richard Petty, who had hit a fence early in the afternoon. He was ready when Pearson veered down the pit lane and clambered out of the Dodge, pawing at his eye. He half-fell, half-climbed over the counter and someone immediately hovered over him with a white handkerchief. Pearson sat gratefully still while three chunks of windshield were scoured out of his eye.

The Dodge wouldn't start. Petty ground ruthlessly on the starter, but the massive engine twisted over without firing. "She's flooded," someone shouted, and a mob of volunteers shoved the car off down the pit lane. Still, nothing, and then one of the pushers spotted a Civil Defense jeep parked near the pits. Shunting the patrolman out of the way, he jumped behind the wheel, crammed it in gear, and shoved it off toward the infield. Moments later the white Dodge appeared, its engine bellowing angrily, and whipped onto the track. The truck was returned to its dumbfounded owner, a crew-cut Canadian named Al, who might have shot and killed anyone else who dared to take his jeep.

It didn't make sense, but Wade had the lead and there wasn't anybody near him. The pit stops for gas were over and only Jarrett was within striking distance. Twenty laps were left when the blue Ford began to close the gap and a wave of excitement swept through the pits. "This may be it. Jarrett's making his move. Wade had better watch it now," someone warned. Jarrett got to within seven seconds of the lead when the engine blew, letting Bill Wade home to win at 98 miles per hour. Petty could not improve on Pearson's position and finished fourth.

Another loss. "Some day, by God, we're gonna win one," said Bud Allman firmly as they loaded the car on the back of the van.

"Not until we get home," said Pearson, the brightness gone from his voice. "Nope. We ain't going no place until we get home. Maybe that'll change our luck."

"We're heading' there tomorrow," said Cotton Owens. "One more race in Pennsylvania and then we'll be back. We get back home and things will be better. You wait and see."

At this point the Cotton Owens racing team and I parted company, and nothing was heard from them until a telegram arrived at the *Car and Driver* office a few days later. It read, "DAVID PEARSON WON HIS FIFTH GRAND NATIONAL RACE HERE AT THE HANOVER, PENNSYLVANIA, DIRT TRACK LAST NIGHT IN A 1964 DODGE. RICHARD PETTY WAS SECOND AND JIMMY PARDUE WAS THIRD." Their luck had changed. They were on the way back home.

It would not change for everyone for the better. During a Goodyear tire test at Charlotte on September 20 Jimmy Pardue, who ranked fourth in the point standing, died when his Dodge Hemi vaulted for the fourth turn wall and crashed heavily. In January 1965 during another test at Daytona, Bill Wade suffered fatal injuries in a mysterious, single-car crash on the superspeedway's second turn, when a tire blew at 170 miles per hour. He would be the fifth NASCAR driver to die within a 12-month period, putting lie to the notion that the big sedans with their roofs and roll bars were safer than open cockpit Indianapolis cars.

When the incredible, grueling, 62-race, coast-to-coast 1964 NASCAR season finally oozed to a halt on November 8, Pearson ended up third in the point standings. He and Owens would win the championship for Dodge in 1966 then, while running for Ford, would gain the title twice again in 1968–1969. When David Pearson retired in 1986 he had won 105 Grand National/Winston Cup races, second only to Richard Petty. He is considered one of the finest stock car drivers of all time.

Chapter Four

TROUBLES IN PARADISE

n retrospect, it would seem that NASCAR has been on a crazy
roll of success and popularity since Bill France and his partners
created the organization in 1947. Yet there have been some nasty
bumps in the road, ugly warfare in the trenches with various automobile manufacturers, drivers, race teams, promoters, and tire
makers, all of whom promoted their unique needs and interests in
the growing sport.

In 1984 President Ronald Reagan witnessed Richard Petty
win his 200th Grand National race at Daytona's July Firecracker
400. It was a win that caused widespread grumbling within the
NACAR fraternity, with other drivers and teams claiming that
Petty's Pontiac was powered by a hugely oversized engine, permitted,
sub rosa, by NASCAR official to assure their greatest star his mile-
stone victory in front of the president. The allegation was never
proved, but would be one of many strange, storybook results,
including Dale Earnhardt's popular victory at the Daytona 500 in
1998 and Jeff Gordon's 1994 triumph in the inaugural Indianapolis
Motor Speedway Brickyard 400. No hard evidence has ever sur-
faced to prove these suspicions, but the performance advantages
enjoyed by Petty, Earnhardt, and Gordon in those three races—as

well as many other "chosen" drivers over years—have left many inside the sport to believe that certain teams at certain times have gotten "the call" beyond the rules in order to hype the show and produce the desired results for the public.

A driver boycott over the feared mega-speeds on the opening of the giant Talladega Speedway in 1969 prompted France himself to climb into a Ford stock car and lap his new track at 175 mph, thereafter claiming to be the "fastest 59 year-old in the world." In doing so he attempted to prove that the track was safe and thereby humiliate his star drivers into participating in the first 500-miler to the held there on September 14, 1969. He failed. With most regulars absent, victory went to relative unknown Richard Brickhouse in a winged Dodge Daytona.

Four years prior to that, France faced another boycott, this time by Chrysler Corporation at his center-piece Daytona 500. Having essentially banned the powerful, all-winning Dodge and Plymouth 426 Hemis from competition following the 1964 season, his February 1965 500 bordered on a flop. With no Chrysler cars, and big-name drivers like Richard Petty and David Pearson absent, France was left with a few front-line Ford teams and a mass of unknowns to fill the field of his most famous and most highly respected race.

France craftily took down bleachers around the circuit, to removing the specter of any empty seats. Still the place looked deserted when I arrived to cover the 500 for *Car and Driver* during the unusually bleak and chilly February of that year. What follows is my report of the race. France, whom I had met briefly during the foray and whom I respected greatly as a brilliant promoter, was not pleased with the story, which attempted to deal with the race as it happened, not as the always ardent tub-thumpers in the NASCAR publicity office would have the public believe.

THE SEVENTH ANNUAL DAYTONA 500
For once, Bill France's magic goose laid a regular egg.

Though a mediocre field of stock cars made it official in a dreary, rain-shortened race, the Ford Motor Company's victory in the seventh annual Daytona 500 actually took place on October 18, 1964. It was on that day that William H.G. France, the homespun paterfamilias of southern auto racing, announced his rules for the 1965 Grand National season and summarily blew any serious Ford opposition clean out of the tub.

Until that moment, the 1965 Daytona 500 was to have been a resumption of the grand conflict between Ford Motor Company and Chrysler Corporation that packed race tracks full of people last year, but the new regulations outlawed the beautifully designed, brutally powerful Chrysler Hemi-head engines and stipulated the use of over-sized Dodge and Plymouth models for competition on the so-called superspeedways. Chrysler reacted with predictable indignation and announced that it would not participate in NASCAR racing in 1965.

This reaction was anticipated by Bill France, a former gas station operator who combined the promotional genius P.T. Barnum with the pride and guts of an Irish heavyweight to become the single most powerful individual to the world of auto racing today. He stubbornly refused to yield to tremendous Chrysler pressure, arguing that his new rules were based on his determination to keep the balance of power on favor of NASCAR rather than the Detroit automakers, and to reduce the cost of competition for the "little guy" in Grand National racing.

France was still on the firing line when race day arrived and sure enough, there wasn't a decent Dodge or Plymouth stock car within 300 miles of Daytona Beach. Though this might be interpreted as a certain moral victory for France and NASCAR—in that he didn't repent and let the Hemis run at the last minute to fill out a weak entry—the fact remains that the race was an artistic bomb that left its winner, Fred Lorenzen, with the limited satisfaction of having beaten five other top-notch Fords, two fast but aged 1964 Mercurys, and 36 of the slowest stock cars this side of Kenosha, Wisconsin.

If the race was any bellwether for the future of the Grand National circuit in 1965—and NASCAR supporters insist that it most decidedly is not—the season may be something less than a box-office smash. As an example, the legions of wild-eyed fans from the Carolinas and Georgia who form the single most important segment of NASCAR race attendance, are apparently irritated over the switch in rules that left hometown favorites like Richard Petty, David Pearson, Bobby Isaac, and Jim Paschal on the sidelines. These good old boys are the stars for Dodge and Plymouth, two makes that have somehow become symbolic underdogs against the massed battalions of the Ford Motor Company.

Thanks to some absurd twists in the black art of image-making, Ford is viewed as a Big Money interloper from the North by many southern racing fans, while they accept the presence of Chrysler—despite its Yankee origins and similarly vast resources—with a certain amount of sympathy. It's all very mysterious, but the fact remains that the fans stayed away from the Daytona 500 in sufficient numbers to cut sharply into the motel and restaurant business in Daytona Beach and to cause an appreciable drop in the race attendance (perfectly evident to anyone who saw the 1964 crowd, despite the absurd "official estimate" of 84,200 people). Add this to the fact that Bill France was roundly booed in his own front yard when he stepped to the microphone during prerace ceremonies, and you can argue that France's laudable ambition to make the Daytona 500 the greatest motor race in the world was definitely not advanced on February 14, 1965.

The quality of the competing automobiles is an excellent standard for judging the success of any race, and, in this context,

Richard Petty on his way to his first Daytona 500 victory in February 1964. This was NASCAR's introduction to the potent Chrysler Hemi engine that dominated Superspeedway competition for the next five years. *Car and Driver archive*

Former motorcycle racing champion Paul Goldsmith takes on fuel for this Plymouth Hemi during the 1964 Daytona 500. He won the pole with a record-shattering speed of 174.910 miles per hour and finished third in the race. *Car and Driver archive*

the Daytona 500 bordered on a disaster. Aside from the 1965 Fords assigned to winner Lorenzen, former winners Junior Johnson and Marvin Panch, veterans Ned Jarrett and Bobby Johns, and a tough newcomer from the rugged IMCA circuit named Dick Hutcherson, there were only two 1964 Mercurys that could be genuinely described as first class automobiles. This pair of machines, beautifully prepared by Bud Moore of Spartanburg, South Carolina, with limited factory aid, came perilously close to embarrassing both Ford and France by winning the biggest stock car race in the world—an honor reserved exclusively for current models. The Mercury driven by affable, hard-luck Darel Dieringer was the fastest in practice, started the race on the pole position, and might have won, had a cut tire not forced an early pit stop. The second Mercury had been planned for Parnelli Jones, but his feud with NASCAR, stemming from a Riverside 500 inspection hassle, caused his withdrawal and the car was turned over to Earl Balmer, a relative newcomer to the big time, who has the matinee-idol looks of A.J. Foyt as well as his bravery.

The rest of the starting field was pitiful, especially if one ponders on the number of big names who were absent from its ranks. In addition to the afore-mentioned Petty and Pearson, the Chrysler battle sidelined Paul Goldsmith, Jim Paschal, and Bobby Isaac. Then there was Jones, A.J. Foyt, Dan Gurney, Jim McElreath, Johnny Rutherford, plus Jo Schlesser, who didn't show up for a variety of reasons, and Fireball Roberts, Jimmy Pardue, Billy Wade, Dave MacDonald, Bobby Marshman, and Larry Thomas, who had lost their lives in the past year. Though the nonappearance of many of these drivers was in many cases, circumstantial, the fact remains that they raced in the 1964 Daytona 500 and they did not race in the 1965 Daytona 500. No one, not even a promotional wizard like Bill France, can have 17 of the biggest names in automobile racing, including five out of six top

1964 500 finishers and the defending champ, sliced out of a starting field and escape unscathed.

As their replacements, NASCAR managed to dredge up a group of drivers so obscure that one wonders if they hadn't been picked through a random canvass of the Daytona Beach phonebook. Fourteen of them were rookies, and several very sharp southern sportswriters who are assigned to stock car racing full time, complained that even they hadn't heard of some of them.

If the drivers were inexperienced nonentities, the cars they were driving were worse. The NASCAR publicity mill tried to get some lineage out of the two 1965 Chevrolets to be driven by Ned Setzer and J.T. Putney, but no one paid much attention. Putney's car was powered by the old 409, which was never effective at Daytona, and Setzer used, of all things, a little ol' 327 (a substitute, he explained, until the 396 becomes available). New Plymouths were entered for Johnny Allen and Buddy Baker, but they were hopelessly outclassed with their 426 "wedge" engines. The remainder of the field was, for the most part, a depressing collection of dented survivors from assorted stock car combats.

An 11-car pileup during one of the two 100-mile qualifying races two days before the 500 added to the vehicle shortage. One of the casualties was the independently entered Oldsmobile of Buck Baker. Certain members of the press permitted themselves the fantasy of writing about the great potential of this car, but the raw facts doomed it from the start. Baker admitted that he had only received the car two-and-a-half weeks before, and about all that had been done to it was to "paint some numbers on her." Before its wreck, the Oldsmobile had taken but a few slow practice laps and by no stretch of the imagination could it have been considered a contender.

To fill out the sparse field (which permits 50 starters, though only 43 finally took the green flag), NASCAR pressed into service a number of tired, slow American Racing Club of America (ARCA) machines that had run a 250-mile race of their own on the high banks the week before.

Fourteen of the casual competitors retired in the first three laps—about the same time the early leader, Junior Johnson, began to lap the field! When the race ended, nearly half of the starters had stopped and most of those running—excepting the leaders—were dawdling around the massive tri-ovals at 125–135 miles per hour.

While most reporters and race officials privately acknowledged the general weakness of the field, they maintained the race itself was outstanding, thanks to the lively scramble for the lead put on by Lorenzen, Panch, and Johnson. In reality, the Daytona Speedway has been the arena for dozens of better races. Junior Johnson, the husky, hill-country folk hero who looks upon lifting one's foot from the throttle as an act of cowardice, put a "hot" 3.23 gear in his Holman-Moody Ford and led the race easily for the first 27 laps. He averaged over 168 miles per hour, while Panch drafted along behind. A cut tire caused Junior to hit the wall and dropped him out of contention. In the meantime, Lorenzen, who was using a 3.1 "drafting" gear that reduced his top speed to 164 miles per hour, but upped gas mileage to a point where he would only have to stop four times instead of the expected five, was tailing Bobby Johns—and falling farther and farther off the leader's pace.

Dieringer was using the same gear ratio as Lorenzen and gambling that he too would be able to draft his way through the race with the leaders. Unfortunately he cut a tire on the eighth lap of the race—probably from a part shed by one of the stragglers—and had to stop at the pits for a fresh left tire. On the 16th lap, third-place man Ned Jarrett encountered a similar failure from alignment troubles that caused his right front tire to rub against the bodywork, and he too had to stop. Both Dieringer and Jarrett ran the race on

Goodyears, which featured an inner-liner for added safety. Dieringer ran four laps on the soft tire before he pitted, and Jarrett made it to the pits at high speed, although the sidewall of the bad tire was nearly scraped off.

Both Firestone and Goodyear had something to crow about after the race. The field was about evenly split on the two brands, and Lorenzen won on Firestones, while Goodyear carried Dieringer to second place.

After Junior Johnson caromed his bright yellow Ford off the wall in the first turn, Marvin Panch took over and led until Bobby Johns nipped past coming off the fourth turn on the 57th lap. But Marvin countered on the back straight and held on until he and Johns made a routine stop on lap 69. Fred Lorenzen inherited the lead as a chill northeast wind picked up velocity, and a gray squadron of clouds swept over the race track.

Panch was back in the lead with Johns second and Lorenzen third by the same time the rain began to fall on lap 80. As the fans in the open grandstands scurried for cover and the infield crowd retreated to their automobiles, the yellow flag came out and the field splashed around the big speedway 22 more times before the all-clear was given.

Following a flurry of pit stops, Lorenzen regained the lead with Panch second and Johns a full circuit back in third. It was on the 127th lap that Fearless Freddy clinched the race. As he slanted into the first turn, with Panch hot on his tail, it began to drizzle slightly, but the two veterans stayed hard on it through the high banks. As they whipped down off the 31-degree slope and onto the back straight, Panch tried to draft by, picking a narrow hole between Lorenzen and the outer wall. Suddenly the rain was pouring down and both men found themselves blinded by water-splashed, oil-smeared windshields. Running nearly 170 miles per hour, Panch nicked the rear bumper of Lorenzen's Ford, and the cars lashed madly out of control. Panch took a wild spin, but somehow avoided hitting anything terribly solid. Lorenzen brushed the wall and bent some sheet metal against his right front tire, but made it into the pits. It took Panch a little longer to get restarted and his hoped for second Daytona win in as many days (he had drafted past Tiny Lund on the final lap to win the Sportsman-Modified 250 the day before) were shot down. He finally finished in sixth place.

After the Lorenzen-Panch tangle, the green flag wasn't seen again. Everybody groped through the falling rain for six more laps, then came to a halt at the finish line. A few loyal fans stood around for an hour waiting for the rain to stop, but the skies remained an uninterrupted slate gray. By the time the race was officially ended at 133 laps, or 332 miles, the grandstands were empty and the stock cars stood alone and neglected on the rain-polished macadam. Lorenzen said after the race that he would like to have "raced to the checker" for the victory, but that lament lasted about five minutes. Fred Lorenzen is too much the professional driver to let artistic achievement stand in the way of a $28,600 payday. The job took him 4 hours and 20 minutes to complete, at the rather modest average speed of 141.539 miles per hour, and that's a pretty favorable hourly wage rate for a former carpenter from Elmhurst, Illinois.

The rain washed away what had been a warm, sunny week of frantic automotive activity for Daytona Beach. From the time ARCA stock cars ran their 250-mile event seven days earlier (won by Michigan grandfather Iggy Katona in a Ford), the famous East Coast beach town of 43,500 vibrated with the noise of racing engines. Each day, intent young men tuned nasty-looking dragsters in motel parking lots for the nightly run-offs at the Spruce Creek Dragstrip outside town. For four warm evenings in a row, the midgets rammed around the narrow, fifth-mile track that bordered the football field in the memorial stadium. And there was the big track. Practice was run daily—though a certain lethargy seemed to be evident—and a pair of 100-mile qualifying races were held two days before the big one. The only interlude of real excitement took pace when LeeRoy Yarbrough took to the track in a 1965 Dodge Hemi fitted with a GMC 6-71 supercharger. He made two attempts to break Art Malone's 181-mile per hour lap record, but mechanical problems slowed him on both occasions. Nevertheless, he was unofficially clocked in the awesomely noisy, 1,000-horsepower brute at 184 miles per hour and did manage to set a new one-lap mark several weeks later. (He ran a 1964 "wedge" Dodge in the race and went nowhere.)

In all, race week was pretty tame compared to last year, when the Fords locked in combat with the Dodges and Plymouths, and even the smallest boy in the grandstands could feel the tension building for the 500-mile race.

Though one sometimes pauses to wonder what roaring flat-out around a 2 1/2-mile tri-oval at 170 miles per hour means (one racing engineer quipped that the track is nothing more than a "circular dynamometer"), the fact remains that lightning speeds, deafening noise, and bumper-to-bumper competition are bywords at the Daytona International Speedway, and these qualities did prevail throughout the bickering, the rain, and the skeletal field that dominated the 1965 500-mile race. Because he has a product of basic appeal to sell the public, it is probable that Bill France will weather the storm that beset his event on February 14. We hope so, because the Daytona 500 deserves the very best cars and drivers the sport can supply.

The big test for NASCAR will come as the Grand National tour makes its way into the southern heartland for such major events as the Atlanta 500, the World 600 at Charlotte, the Southeastern 500 at Bristol, and the Darlington 500. It is here that Bill France will learn the overall effect his new rules have had on the sport. Florida is considered to be alien territory to most of the NASCAR people, although its headquarters are located in Daytona Beach. The geographical center of stock car racing is probably located somewhere near Spartanburg, South Carolina, and it was there, not Daytona Beach, that the vast base of enthusiasm developed for Grand National competition. A Holman-Moody mechanic summed it up when he said, "I never did like Daytona Beach and I can't wait until we all back up south." It is "up south" where the verdict will be handed down.

Chapter Five

DAYTONA 1966:
ALMOST A RUNAWAY FOR RICHARD

The middle 1960s seemed to generate an endless series of disputes within the NASCAR crowd. Trying to herd this mob of angry cats was ringleader Bill France, Jr., who never seemed to get the act totally together. His problems were based entirely on the divergent and increasingly ardent demands of the biggies from Ford and Chrysler lurking in the background, who were constantly at loggerheads over the rules that theoretically required that their "stock" cars compete on the Grand National Circuit.

This was akin to expecting America's Cup competitors to show up in rowboats purchased from Sears Roebuck. As the stakes rose and the mantra, "Win on Sunday, sell on Monday," gained strength, especially in the South, the manufacturers began to invest more money and talent into winning major races like the Daytona 500, the Charlotte World 600, the Daytona Firecracker 400, and the Darlington Southern 500.

Money and brains stimulated creativity and the inevitable fudging of the rules, if not outright cheating. France was in the middle, frantically juggling in order to keep the competition even while Chrysler built full-race Hemis and Ford responded with exotic, race-only V-8s of its own.

Not only were the manufacturers and their race teams working hard to develop more horsepower, but aerodynamics were beginning to play a role. For most of the century, race cars of all kinds limited "aero" to simple streamlining. But in the mid-1960s small wings and airfoils were beginning to appear, not to slicken the body shapes, but to create negative down force to enhance adhesion in the corners. This would slowly lead to the ground-effects revolution a decade later, but as the 1966 Daytona 500 opened the NASCAR season, a number of teams had begun to make subtle improvements on the stock bodywork, not only to reduce drag, but to produce more stability on the speedway's high banks.

Pandora's box had been opened, and not even Bill France could close it. I wrote the following story, which was published in the May 1966 issue of *Car and Driver*. Again, its irreverent tone rustled feathers in the NASCAR headquarters in Daytona Beach:

DAYTONA BEACH:
February 1966

When Richard Petty isn't buckled into the seat of his father's bright blue Plymouth stock car, he smiles a lot and talks pleasantly in a Carolina drawl so thick you could stir it with a spoon. He is a genuinely kind and unassuming young man, and the stock car fans from Roanoke to Charlotte love him like no other race driver. Uniquely, he is also held in great esteem by his NASCAR competitors, who seem to bear him no grudge even though he consistently drives faster than they do. They also respect his father, Lee, and his brother, Maurice, the two next most important members of the great Randleman, North Carolina, Petty clan. Lee is a former Grand National stock car driver—one of the two or three all-time best—and Maurice is the chief mechanic on the Plymouths Richards drives. He tried racing himself for a while, but gave it up several years ago and now seems perfectly content to make his brother's cars go farther and faster than anybody else's. And Maurice does this effectively, while ol'Lee acts as the convivial boss of the whole shootin'match.

Can this mean that nice guys do win? Yes, apparently, though the Pettys effectively substitute hours of work and careful planning for any generic nastiness that might be necessary in an equation for victory. When the Pettys arrive at a race, they are always ready to unload their tough-looking Number 43 Plymouth from its transporter and hit competitive speeds after maybe 15 minutes of practice. They have learned the lesson of proper preparation, and no other race in their long, victory-packed career is a better example than the eighth annual Daytona 500, run recently around the precipitous macadam banks of Bill France's great swampland monument to high speed commerce.

Richard, Lee, and Maurice were among the first to arrive at Daytona when practice opened several weeks prior to the race, and they looked ready to run 500 miles on a moment's notice. The car they brought along was the result of lengthy pondering over the NASCAR Grand National rules, and it took advantage of some obvious loopholes in the regulations regarding streamlining. The Plymouth's windshield was canted back slightly and its entire front fender and hood sections were sloped down to present a more aerodynamic shape to the 180-mile per hour Daytona air currents. Prevented from defending their 1964 Daytona victory in 1965 due to a hassle between Chrysler Corporation and Bill France over the legality of the famous Hemi engines, the Pettys returned this year with an iron-clad resolve to make up for lost time. The truce between Chrysler and France resulted in a set of compromise terms that forced intermediate sizes cars like the Plymouth Belvederes and the Dodge Chargers to race with 405-ci engines. Because they were running larger-wheelbase Galaxies, the new rules permitted the Fords to compete with 427-ci engines, and this 22-ci handicap had the Pettys so concerned that they turned to aerodynamics for more speed.

Their solution to the problem, and the imitators it spawned, caused the first of several flaps that swirled around Lee and Richard during the Daytona 500, but they kept smiling through it all, oblivious to the foot-stamping and the teeth-gnashing that was going on. Conflicts come naturally to the Daytona International Speedway, and it is difficult to recall a 500-miler in which bickering didn't mar the proceedings. This year the trouble involved first the streamlining and finally, tires, but these were only momentary distractions for Richard, Lee, and Maurice as they picked up their second win in as many tries, averaging a record-breaking 160 miles per hour along the way.

The conflict that superseded all others at Daytona took place between the Ford Motor Company and the Chrysler Corporation and was carried out with superficial, big-business sportsmanship and good will. These two giants are both aware that most of the promotional ammunition to be collected from stock car racing comes at the Daytona 500. Officials of both companies candidly admit that they would not trade a victory at Daytona for wins in all of the other major NASCAR events, and this means that millions are expended annually to get this checkered flag. Last year, Ford had the place to itself, thanks to the Chrysler ban, and won a race that offered about as much prestige as Italy's Ethiopian campaign.

Ford returned this year knowing full well that its three-year-old 427 V-8, even with its displacement advantage, would be hard-pressed to keep up with the power-packed 405 Hemi. Lamented a Ford man prior to the race, "But we're all hoping that the smaller Hemis will be down on reliability, because they'll have to rev' em higher." That was the first of many disappointments for the Ford forces, because the de-stroked Hemis ran with the speed and dependability of Japanese trains. As it turned out, the Fords had to wind to 7,200 rpm while the Hemis were loafing along at 6,800. "The

405 Hemi is just as powerful as the old 426 version, though it is down slightly on torque," said a Chrysler representative shortly before the race. "But, hell, Daytona is a track that demands raw horsepower, so who needs torque?"

Richard Petty didn't need much, apparently, because he began bustling around the big oval at over 175 miles per hour almost from the moment he hit the track for practice. The other big Chrysler guns were driving cars prepared by the highly respected Ray Nichels Engineering operation, but because boss Ray Nichels hadn't gotten the word about the cute stuff that could be done with streamlining, Plymouth drivers Paul Goldsmith and Jim Hurtubise weren't immediately competitive. Added to Nichels' initial woes were some engine valve train problems that finally forced Ray to pack up his cars during the second week of practice and head back to Griffith, Indiana, for some major updating.

As practice began to get serious, only one Ford was getting around Daytona in impressive fashion, and that was a bronze, droop-nose vehicle driven by Dick Hutcherson. Like Petty's, it had received extensive custom work on the front end, which was paying off with speeds over 175 miles per hour. Because maybe 98 percent of all racing engineering, both here and abroad, operates on the monkey-see, monkey-do principle, the Petty and Hutcherson streamlining efforts sent everybody back to the garage to saw and hack on the noses and windshields of their automobiles.

Some of the cars reappeared looking more suitable for a run at the Land Speed Record than for competition in the Daytona 500, so ol' Bill France decided to put his foot down about streamlining. France, who sometimes promulgates and supersedes more rules in a given week than the Postal Department does in 10 years, came out four-square in favor of stock cars by ruling that bodywork could only be lowered 4 inches below the original Detroit dimensions.

Paper and debris scatter as the 1964 Daytona 500 begins. The Hemi-powered Plymouths of Richard Petty and Paul Goldsmith are already out in front. *Car and Driver archive*

Richard Petty stops on his way to victory in the 1964 Daytona 500. Crew chief and cousin Dale Inman (right) gives Petty hand signals as he reaches for a cup of water. Note the debris that has accumulated on the front grille-work and the small grandstands in the background. *Car and Driver archive*

Defending NASCAR
champion Ned Jarrett at the
wheel of his Ford during
the 1966 World 600
at Charlotte. A cerebral,
consistent driver, Jarrett ran
to finish, as opposed to the
hard-charging tactics
employed by his rivals Junior
Johnson, David Pearson,
and Curtis Turner. Jarett
would go on to a long career
in broadcasting following his
retirement from competition.
Don Hunter

Thus reassured that Bill France wasn't going to let anyone tamper with the rules, the entrants redoubled their efforts toward extracting speed by more conventional means.

Meanwhile the Nichels cars had returned from Indiana and Paul Goldsmith found the speed he had been seeking. Deciding there was no time left to set up his 1966 Plymouth, Paul discarded it in favor of the 1965 machine that had carried him to third place in the Riverside 500, and suddenly found himself unwinding laps at 177 miles per hour. Jim Hurtubise, who had only run Daytona once before, was almost as fast, and, except for Hutcherson, the Ford camp was plunged into gloom. The two Wood Brothers' cars, driven by veterans Marvin Panch and Curtis Turner, were running in the low 170s, as was the Holman-Moody machine of star Fred Lorenzen, and the Banjo Matthews-entered car piloted by sensational young Cale Yarborough.

Two Holly Farms cars owned by good old boy Junior Johnson were going slower every day, and the garage area crowd was openly relishing the heavyweight match they figured would erupt between Johnson and his superstar driver, A.J Foyt. Foyt rejected two of Junior's cars as too slow before settling for a Ford that Jack Bowsher had driven to victory in the ARCA 250-miler a week before. Foyt went little faster in his third machine, while relations between himself and his boss got downright surly. "Maybe we oughta quit worryin' about switchin' cars an' start switchin' drivers," drawled a Johnson man late in the week. But Foyt and Johnson somehow managed to keep their tempers, and A.J did drive in the race—though in compete obscurity until the car broke on the 46th lap.

While the rather boxy Plymouths were shattering records, the mechanically similar but slipperier-shaped Dodge Chargers were having trouble reaching competitive speeds. Most prerace speculation centered on how much quicker the fastback Chargers would be than the rest of the field, but it soon became apparent that simply too many handling mysteries had to be solved before they would be contenders. The three Charger drivers, David Pearson, LeeRoy Yarbrough, and Sam McQuagg, were convinced that the tails of the cars were lifting in the corners—which caused a great rash of tongue-wagging around the pits—until Dodge engineers traced the entire problem to the suspensions. It was finally decided that too much simple but time-consuming development work remained to be done on the Chargers, and all three were fitted with "cruising" gears for the race to provide better gas mileage and reliability. "They aren't going to win this one, but I hate to think about how fast they'll have 'em going by the time we get back here for the Firecracker 400," moaned a Ford official.

The pair of 100-mile qualifying races that were run two days before the 500 turned out much as expected, with the Hemis tromping the field. Goldsmith, who the day before had cranked off three consecutive laps at over 177 miles per hour, followed by one at an unprecedented 178 miles per hour, won the first race. Earl Balmer, driving a 1965 Dodge, took the other. Both men pulled the old Daytona trick of "sling-shotting" off the fourth turn on the final lap and blasting past the helpless leader in a swirl of turbulent air. Goldsmith was able to turn his trick with none other than Richard Petty, while Balmer nipped Hutcherson, who crunched the wall during the maneuver and finished third behind Jim Hurtubise.

This left one day for everybody to establish some sort of strategy for winning, and it was obvious that the Ford drivers—excepting Hutcherson—would try to run a steady, fuel-conserving pace and pray fervently that the Plymouths would blow up or waste too much time in the pits. Aside from an awful, almost unbelievable twist of fate, this tactic might have worked, because men like Turner, Panch, Cale Yarborough, and Lorenzen drove beautifully disciplined races and might well have finished better.

The great tire debacle, which changed the entire complexion of the race and almost cost Petty his victory, began during practice when some minor chunking (throwing sections of tread at high speed) developed on the soft-compound Goodyear tires. Petty had qualified for the pole position on Firestone tires, but switched to Goodyear for the race, claiming that they gave him better handling in a wider selection of grooves. The Goodyear people were privately apprehensive about the possibility of their new tires chunking (they had been introduced with less testing than hoped for), but they counted on caution flags and the continuation of Daytona's cool, damp weather on race day to aid tire wear.

Lest there be any misunderstanding, one of the biggest rivalries in sports exists between the Goodyear and Firestone tire companies, and there was widespread head-shaking and eye-rolling in the Firestone camp about what was going to happen to the men on Goodyears. They were absolutely correct in predicting the Goodyears would chunk, but not one Firestone man in his wildest, most paranoid nightmares, ever dreamed that the Goodyear troubles might cost Firestone its chance of winning!

On the 11th lap, Jarrett changed a pair of Goodyears. The word passed down pit row like a Hollywood rumor: Jarrett's tires had chunked! A few moments later, Darrel Dieringer brought his ancient but active 1964 Mercury in with the same problem, and the battle for the lead suddenly assumed tremendous significance. Petty and Goldsmith were out in front, alternating the lead at a furious 175-mile per hour pace, while Jim Hurtubise was holding off Dick Hutcherson, a short distance behind. Goldsmith, Petty, and Hurtubise were on Goodyears, and Hutcherson was on the slower but longer-wearing harder compound Firestone tires.

Tough Ronney Householder, the ex-midget racing champion who now runs the nuts-and-bolts end of the Chrysler racing program, immediately realized the potential danger in the situation: If his Plymouths had to make one or two extra stops for tires, their extra speed would be nullified in the face of the steady-paced Fords. At the same time, Leo Beebe, the patrician FoMoCo racing boss, began to see hope building for his boys. Panch, Turner, Yarborough, and Lorenzen were all in the front echelon—and they too were running Firestones.

Beebe's first trauma occurred on the 38th lap. Dick Hutcherson came roaring down the pit lane and stopped with an ugly web of cracks spread across his windshield. His crew laid some tape across the rupture, but a NASCAR official called them off and thumbed the car out of the race. Hutcherson was justifiably angry, because his windshield had been smashed by a flying chunk of rubber from Jim Hurtubise's left rear tire. Beebe stoically lit a long, expensive cigar. Hutcherson's departure was a grievous blow to the Ford campaign. The fastest of the entire FoMoCo team, Hutcherson was fully prepared to run the race at a 172–173-mile per hour average—a speed, as it turned out, that would have put him in the thick of the battle at the end. But the day wasn't entirely lost for Ford: at that point Richard Petty got the signal from his crew to come in.

Petty stopped and Maurice and Lee and the rest of the crew leapt over the wall to yank off a smoking set of Goodyears with gaping holes chewed in the threads. By the time he got back into traffic, Richard was over a lap behind. Elsewhere along the pits, panic set in and a number of drivers, including A.J. Foyt, changed from Goodyear to Firestone on the spot. Petty's powerful Hemi quickly brought him back into contention, and while normal stops for gasoline and tires jumbled the order, Richard managed to maintain command for much of the early running. However, Marvin Panch and Cale Yarborough were within easy striking distance of the three leaders.

Back in the speedway garage area, the Firestone and Goodyear crews were working like demons—the Goodyear men hustling to change the new tires for a proven, harder compound version, while their rivals gleefully yanked Goodyears off the spare wheels of various cars and replaced them with Firestones. One of the crew chiefs who sent a set of wheels to the Firestone garage was Lee Petty, who had decided that too much was at stake to maintain blind loyalty to Goodyear. Four mounted Firestones actually arrived in the Petty pit and were set for installation on Richard's next stop when a Goodyear man appeared with a set of their harder tires. The Petty family composure broke down briefly while Maurice and his father argued about which brand to use, but the Goodyear forces prevailed and Richard went on to the finish the race with their tires. The harder compound cut about 3 miles per hour off his top speed, but the 172-and 173-mile per hour laps he was turning were still sufficient to hold the remaining Fords at bay.

On the 119th lap, Panch arrived at his pit with his windshield looking as if somebody had heaved a brick at it. As in the case of Hutcherson, NASCAR officials ruled the car unsafe for competition, and Marvin was through for the afternoon. Flying rubber had done it, and again the culprit was Hurtubise. "It happened some time ago." Said Panch, "and at first it wasn't too bad. Then the vibration and air pressure made it worse and there wasn't anything I could do."

"It was Hurtubise," drawled Curtis Turner. "He got me an' Marvin an' Hutcherson with the rubber flyin' off his tars." The Ford people were going up the wall. Three cars—three good cars, running like clock-work, knocked out like ten-pins by one guy. A Plymouth guy at that! The Firestone representatives felt equally jinxed, because now only Cale Yarborough had a chance of winning with their brand, though Hurtubise did them a small favor—and added a final twist of irony to the tread-throwing incident.

As it was, Hurtubise paid for his mischief. Though he ran as fast as anybody on the track, the chunking tires and the ensuing change of brands cost him so much time in the pits that he could finish no higher than sixth. The tire problem also dropped Goldsmith out of contention. After making several stops, the Nichels crew shod the Plymouth with harder-compound Goodyears, but Paul complained that they ruined the handling and still another time-consuming switch was made to Firestones. It was all for naught anyway, because the car broke a U-joint late in the race and Goldsmith tumbled all the way to 18th in the final standings.

As the race spun into its final laps, an ominous black rain cloud rolled over the track. Richard Petty was running comfortably in front of Cale Yarborough, who in turn led steady, but slow-running Lorenzen and Pearson. The whole affair had become a procession when the rain began to fall six laps from the finish. The NASCAR people let the boys fly blind—minus rain tires or windshield wipers—for two more circuits before waving the yellow flag. This, for all intents, ended the race. They splashed through the downpour for another two laps and then the race was called, five miles early.

An empty gas tank forced Lorenzen to stop moments before the end, letting David Pearson into third place, but otherwise the Daytona 495 ended with a minimum of thrills. Had Cale Yarborough not lost a full lap earlier in the race by overshooting his pit during a routine stop, the end might have been extremely thrilling—and possibly more satisfying to the Ford group. But as it was, how could a Ford man expect anything better on such a foul, rotten-luck day? (They probably should have been thankful that the Goodyear balloon hadn't fallen out of the sky on top of Yarborough and Lorenzen.)

Despite all of the silly switches and tricks of fate, one ringing fact remained after the sound and the fury died down; the Pettys came to the race with a superior organization and a superior car, and they simply overpowered their opponents. Bad luck helped beat the Fords, but in the final analysis, the thing that did them in was a big, loose-limbed kid from North Carolina and his family's ol' blue Plymouth. And for Ronney Householder and the men at Chrysler, that's all that really mattered.

THE FRENCH CONNECTION

In this day of cloned race cars, androgynous, carefully templated bodywork, and tightly regulated engines, dense-pack stock car racing is the order of the day. Most races are decided by a car length or less on the final lap. This was not always the case in days when various makes, with their stock bodies (presumably) and different powerplants often had wide advantages. Add to that the nuance of cheating that had been elevated to a high art by race car builders and mechanics, and races were often runaways for one type of car or another.

In order to keep the competition close, yellow flags were arbitrarily flown to reduce speeds and to reform the field into a bumper-to-bumper line-up for the restart. These caution periods were often announced as being caused by debris on the track, although observers at trackside and in the press box could see nothing that might cause a hazard. This prompted a long-forgotten jokester among the press corps to identify a mysterious French driver named "Pierre Debris." When a caution was waved by NASCAR officials for no apparent reason other than to tighten the competition, a cry would often go up in the press box, "Pierre Debris is on the track!"

Chapter Six

A WESTERN PLAYGROUND

While NASCAR racing had exploded in the southeast during the 1960s, California remained a hotbed of hot rodding, drag racing, sprints, and midget competition and a cauldron of enthusiasm for sports cars. Roadracing had begun in the early 1950s on open roads near stylish locations like Pebble Beach and Torrey Pines, but soon gave way to permanent circuits at Riverside in the south and Laguna Seca on the Monterey Peninsula in the center of the vast state.

Riverside, opened in 1957, grew to be one of the most important and prestigious race tracks in the nation until expanding populations and soaring real estate values forced it out of business in 1988. But in the 1960s Riverside was at its peak, the site of the second United States Grand Prix for Formula 1 cars in 1960 and the annual *Los Angeles Times* Grand Prix for sports cars that attracted crowds of over 100,000. So too for the *Motor Trend* 500 for NASCAR cars, an event that became one of the most popular and lucrative races on the grueling cost-to-coast schedule for the Dixie-based teams.

In a rare bit of cooperation between various competing organizations, the *Motor Trend* race attracted the best and brightest from NASCAR, as well as Indy stars like A.J. Foyt, Parnelli Jones, and Dan Gurney. The latter, perhaps the finest roadracing driver ever produced in the United States, dominated the race from 1963 to 1966, winning four times in a row until Parnelli Jones broke his streak in 1967.

It was during Gurney's victory drive in 1966 that he engaged in one of the fiercest duels of his long career, with Curtis Turner, who had returned from a "lifetime suspension" by Bill France after attempting to enlist the Teamsters Union to organize the drivers. Turner, whose brilliance behind the wheel still registers awe among veterans 30 years following his death, was not considered a natural roadracing driver, having spent his career on the rough ovals of the South. But it was forgotten that he had honed his skills driving bootleg hooch over the hills of Virginia, and his expertise on the twisties was staggering.

Turner appeared at Riverside in 1966 as part of the Wood Brothers Team, a team that also included Gurney in a sister Ford. The two men got along famously, despite their disparate backgrounds. Prior to the race, Turner invited Gurney to a party where he noted the place would be full of his favored "baby dolls" and plenty of "shooters" for everyone. Dan demurred, telling Turner that he never drank prior to a race. Turner smiled and said in his slow Virginia drawl, "Dan you've got it all wrong. The only way to race is with a damn ol' hangover. That way, you feel so bad you don't give a shit what happens to you."

A tradition at the *Motor Trend* race was a preevent party held at the famed, historic Mission Inn in nearby Riverside. Drivers, crew members, press types, and Hollywood celebrities were on hand for the festivities. During the evening a buxom young movie bimbo named Edie Williams, who starred in such bombs as *Beyond the Valley of the Dolls*, began speaking with Turner. Williams asked, "Do you smoke a cigar while you race?"

Turner, peering into her creamy cleavage, took a sip of his Canadian Club and Coke, and replied softly, "No, but I will."

On the other side of the crowded room, young Buddy Baker was being interviewed by a television reporter from Los Angeles. Baker, a young giant and the son of NASCAR pioneer driver Buck Baker, was just beginning his long and fruitful career. Known for his hard driving and his droll sense of humor, Buddy Baker would retire with the 1980 Daytona 500 victory under his belt and begin a long career of race commentary in the television booth. The reporter, a young woman who knew nothing about the sport, asked, "Mr. Baker, where are you from?"

"I'm from Charlotte, North Carolina."

"Oh really," replied the woman. "Now where would that be?" One must recall that in 1966 Charlotte was a dot on the map. Its largest hotel was the "Heart of Charlotte" Motel. It would be another decade before the city would explode in growth and prosperity and became one of the best-known, most attractive cities in the nation.

"Well," said Baker after a long pause, Charlotte is about half way between Concord and Gastonia."

The answer seemed to satisfy the LA reporter, and she went on to other more salient questions. Surely within her lifetime she would more than understand where the Queen City of Charlotte was located.

The 1966 *Motor Trend* 500 was yet another victory for Dan Gurney, although not until Turner's Ford had expired, following one of the greatest duels in the history of stock car racing. Turner raced with Gurney at the very highest level of car control. Gurney later reflected on his rival's driving: "At one point we got into the esses almost side by side. Then Curtis lost it. He got off the track and into the sand. Somehow he regained control in an impossible situation. It was amazing. I don't think there were five drivers in the entire world who could have recovered in a situation like that. He was one of the greatest of all time, in my opinion."

I watched that mad duel during my first exposure to NASCAR Grand National stars cavorting on a road course since my travels with David Pearson at Bridgehampton and Watkins Glen two years earlier. I wrote the following story for *Car and Driver*, and it appeared in the April 1966 issue. Keep in mind that many drivers who would later become household words among racing fans were essentially unknown in 1966. The story treats such future greats as Mario Andretti and Cale Yarborough as young newcomers, not truly capable of running with the big boys like Turner, Gurney, and Pearson. That would of course change almost before the ink was dry on this story. The piece also mentions heroic Jim Hurtubise, who drove at Riverside with incredible courage despite the horrific burns on his hands suffered the year before in a crash at Milwaukee—an incident still fresh in the minds of the magazine's readers at that time, but now long forgotten:

Dan's Own Race—The Riverside 500

Ned Jarrett was in the men's room behind the pits at Riverside, rubbing off 500 miles' worth of dirt and rubber accumulated while manhandling a sick stock car over the 2.7-mile road course. "This race is murder," the two-time NASCAR champ said. "They're the toughest 500 miles we drive every year; tougher than Atlanta, tougher than Daytona, even tougher than Darlington. Man, I'm exhausted."

Meanwhile, across the dusk-shrouded track, Dan Gurney sat comfortably in a big leather chair in the new administration building, surrounded by members of the adoring local press. Gurney had just soundly thrashed a field of expert southern stock car drivers—including Jarrett—and now he was enjoying a moment's relaxation before picking up his $20,380 first-place money and taking a brief freeway drive to his Costa Mesa home.

For the fourth time in four years, Dan Gurney had won the Riverside 500, and in so doing had beaten one of the finest fields of racing stars ever gathered together outside Indianapolis or Daytona. His victory had come despite the all-out efforts of tough pros like David Pearson and Curtis Turner, who trailed him throughout the race like hungry wolves and now stood silently in the darkness while their battered cars were being loaded aboard transporters. Junior Johnson, whose two cars, driven by A.J. Foyt and Bobby Isaac, had been forced out of the race early, summed up the NASCAR efforts in the face of Dan Gurney's expertise at Riverside when he grumbled, "We got about as much business bein' here as a one-legged man in an ass-kicking contest."

It had been Pearson who had come closest to breaking Gurney's hold on the race. He had run the 500 miles in perfect discipline, limiting his rpm to preserve the Hemi engine in his 1965 Dodge, and specifically avoiding any car-breaking duels. Pearson had taken the pole position at a record-breaking 106.078 miles per hour and had led the early stages. He lapped the course quickly and cleanly, with as much authority as Gurney, but bad luck in the pits nullified his chance of winning. Aside from each of his stops being slightly longer than Gurney's, Pearson lost precious seconds when he was released from a gasoline stop without a filler cap and was black-flagged a lap later to get it replaced. To make matters worse, he and Paul Goldsmith had a minor shunt in the pits during an earlier stop and the cumulative loss of time meant 1 minute and 14 seconds disadvantage at the end of the race. "We woulda bet anything that Gurney wasn't going to finish," said a member of the Pearson crew. "We figured the Fords weren't going to last, and we played the waitin' game for the whole race. I guess we waited too long."

Curtis Turner didn't wait, but he lost anyway. In his first Riverside race after a lengthy suspension by NASCAR for trying to

Junior Johnson makes a pit stop on his way to victory at Darlington in May 1965 in his Holley Farms Ford. The brilliant, ex-bootlegging driver won 10 of the 36 Grand National races that year and was the subject of a Tom Wolfe story in Esquire titled "The Last American Hero," which subsequently became a major motion picture.
Don Hunter

NASCAR officials try to measure the record-breaking Smokey Yunick/Curtis Turner Chevelle prior to the 1967 Daytona 500. The car had been artfully sculpted to a point where it was actually a 7/8-scale replica of the original. This marked the first time templates were employed, mainly because of clever bodywork fabricated by master craftsmen like Yunick. *Car and Driver archive*

organize a driver's union, Turner took to the twisty course immediately. "Hell, road racin' is just like runnin' whiskey—and that's how I learned to drive," said Turner prior to the race. The most legendary stock car driver of them all—including Junior Johnson and Fireball Roberts—Curtis Turner is a shambling giant of a man who acts about as competitive as Smokey the Bear when he's not behind the wheel. But all that changes when the racing begins. Curtis Turner is one of the most skillful, tenacious drivers in the history of the sport, and it was at Riverside that he demonstrated that none of his vaunted ability had been dissipated during his forced retirement. While Pearson played the waiting game with Gurney, Turner assaulted the champ with everything except a lead pipe. Both of them were driving Fords prepared by the canny Wood brothers of Stuart, Virginia, and the entire clan was a study in deep concern as they witnessed their two team members flailing away at each other for lap after lap. They tried to slow them down on several occasions, but it was no use, and the struggle ended only when Turner made a pit stop. The dice was a high point of the race for the 72,000 Californians who showed up, though Gurney admitted later that the battle wasn't quite as grim as it looked. "We were running faster than we should have been, but not as fast as we could have," he said.

Turner crunched a fence in the later stages of the race, and that put him out of contention for good. He roared into the pits with his left front fender crumpled beyond recognition and squirmed impatiently in his seat while the Wood brothers cut the ruined metal away from the tire. An unscheduled stop for gasoline a short time later and a nasty spin trying to avoid a slow-running Jack McCoy dropped him to fourth place at the end. For a while, Leonard and Glen and the other Wood boys had their team running 1-2-3, with Gurney leading Marvin Panch and Turner, but that all ended when Panch's transmission blew, and he retired on lap 50.

While everyone was keeping track of Gurney and his pur-
suers, Paul Goldsmith was running steadily toward a completely
unheralded third-place finish. A first-rank driver of stock cars, the
taciturn ex-motorcycle champion has not enjoyed a particularly consistent finishing record in recent years, despite the fact that he has
been the Number One man for Chrysler Corp. specialist Ray
Nichels. Some people have attributed Goldsmith's low finishing
average to a poor sense of pace, whereby he runs a car flat out until
something breaks. True or not, Goldsmith had no chance to run his
Plymouth on the limit in the Riverside 500, owing to a faulty secondary carburetor throat that refused to open no matter how hard Paul
mashed down the throttle. This ailment cut his top speed considerably,
but it may have contributed to his high finish.

A total of 44 cars started the race, although only a third of
them could be taken seriously. Obviously, the hot stuff was restricted
to the factory Dodges, Plymouths, and Fords. Sports car expert Jerry
Grant was on hand with a neatly prepared '65 Chevy 427 that ran
with the front echelon of factory cars until the three lower gears in
his transmission disappeared. Up to that point, Grant had been
motoring around the track—with which he is extremely familiar—in
impressive fashion. But with only fourth gear remaining, he put-
tered steadily to the finish, staying out of the way of the faster cars.
Near the end, when he had 11th place sewed up, but was obviously
going to do no better, his crew lavishing hard, hung out a sign that
said, "Grant, make your move."

A grand display of guts was forthcoming from Jim Hurtubise,
who somehow kept his bleeding, scarred hands on the wheel long
enough to capture sixth place. A man who runs wide open or not at
all, Hurtubise put on a stirring demonstration of big car wrestling
for most of the race's five-hour duration. He thrust his white, Norm
Nelson-prepared Plymouth from a midpack starting position up

among the leaders in the early stages and stayed there throughout the afternoon. His driving wasn't the tidiest on the track, but it was at all times spectacular, and Hurtubise established himself an impressive following within the crowd before the end.

Don White, the Iowa veteran of the USAC stock car circuit, covered himself with glory at Riverside. A minor member of the cast when the race began, White calmly drove away from a mob of head-liners and had third place firmly in hand when the engine in his Ray Nichels Dodge blew up. His departure also forced the exit of USAC National Champion Mario Andretti. White spilled oil on the track when his engine disintegrated, Andretti spun, and their cars collided in the confusion. This incident was the last in a series of frustrations for the youthful Andretti that spanned both practice and the race. He was prevented from making a qualifying run on the first day of trials when NASCAR officials discovered that the windshield of his new Ford lacked the necessary safety clamps. He finally made the starting field, though his car was far from a potential winner. There are, and have been, a fair number of so-called American and Euro-pean "champions" who would've refused to run back in the ruck, the way Andretti did at Riverside. Being the reigning USAC national champ, the kid easily might have rationalized himself out of driving with the nobodies and parked the car, but Andretti isn't that kind of competitor. He spun three times in the race, once when a slower car cut him off in the esses, once through sheer exuberance and once when he and White clouted each other. But he hung in until the bitter end, and for that he deserves great credit.

Of less distinction was the performance of the man Andretti succeeded as national champion—ol' A.J. Foyt. After surviving a lusty slam against the Turn One fence during practice ("I always wondered if you take it flat out—now I know you gotta breathe her a little.") Foyt drove his Junior Johnson-prepared Ford around for a few laps and then turned it over to Darel Dieringer, who struggled onward until the transmission quit at 48 laps. Foyt told the press that a bad head cold prompted his retirement, but cynics felt it was a lack of speed, rather than health, that caused it. David Pearson, whose boyish enthusiasm for racing is widely known, reported passing Foyt on the back stretch and trying to egg him on with a great display of arm waving, but got nothing for his trouble but a gloomy "thumbs down" signal from the tough Texan. A few laps later Foyt quit.

In among the stars in the starting field were two youthful NASCAR talents who—due to car troubles—never really got a chance to shine. Richard Petty normally mounts a tremendous challenge on road circuits, but his Plymouth never ran properly all week and he was forced out of the running when his engine blew on the 105th lap. Cale Yarborough, a barrel-chested lad from Timmonsville, South Carolina, who is starting his first season in a really first-class car, ran very rapidly in the opening laps—recording the fastest straightaway speed at 148 miles per hour in the process—but his transmission packed up after 103 laps, and he was out.

Petty's and Yarborough's fortunes were only slightly better than Fred Lorenzen's, who didn't even make the starting line-up due to a nasty crackup in practice. He lost control of his Holman-Moody Ford in the treacherous Turn One and flipped end-over-end numerous times across the reclaimed desert before coming to rest. His car was completely destroyed, though he escaped with minor bruises. Fred was working out the kinks in his Elmhurst, Illinois, home by the time the race began.

Actually, he didn't miss much, at least in terms of sheer spine-tingling excitement. Despite all the thrashing around, Dan Gurney maintained cool command of the race for a substantial percentage of the distance and therefore any gnawing suspense over who was going to win was absent. The appeal of the Riverside 500 was based on that overall spectacle of witnessing a mob of brightly colored, bellowing automobiles gamboling over the countryside like a herd of runaway steers. Stock car roadracing is in fact like a mechanical stampede, and we personally think it's maybe the neatest form of motor racing known to man. It's definitely the greatest spectacle in roadracing.

After the racket had been absorbed by the rocky hills surrounding Riverside, and the multitudes had snarled themselves into a massive traffic jam on the San Bernardino Freeway, the vivid recollection of Dan Gurney's virtuosity dominated all other memories of the event. Gurney is a big man—so big that he somehow looks outsized for the effete Formula One cars in which he has gained most of his fame. But he is perfectly suited for the spacious cockpit of a stock car and this, added to his bold, confident driving style, makes him uniquely qualified for this brand of competition. There are moments in motor racing that stand out due to certain visual or audible assaults on the senses—when the spectator knows instinctively that he is witnessing something unforgettable. One of these moments comes when Gurney charges through the blind, reverse camber Turn One at Riverside and thunders flat out in third gear into the esses. Dust flies and tires howl as his car slews along the verge of the track, seemingly on the outer limits of control. He is perceptibly faster than anyone else through this series of bends, and the sight of him, sitting bolt upright behind the wheel of his monstrous race car, is not one that is easily ignored.

Because most of the big guns in stock car racing save their heavy artillery for the Daytona 500, the Riverside go-round isn't much of a bellwether for the upcoming season, but that in no way limits its appeal. As the West Coast's only major stock car event, it lives up to its billing as one of the most important motor races in the United States. And when one considers that it is only four years old, its growth is all the more phenomenal. And this year the capricious and evil-tempered gods who control the weather in that desert outpost relented and gave the crowd warm temperatures, clear skies, and modest winds in which to view the race. Such an event only creates the desire for more road-races like it across the nation—and additional opportunities to see Mr. Gurney and his peers have at it again.

Chapter Seven

GO LEEROY:
A WILD RIDE AT DAYTONA

I t will be remembered as the Tire War. For most of the 1960s
Goodyear and Firestone engaged in a vicious, multimillion dollar conflict to dominate motor racing, both here and abroad. The
battle raged at the highest levels, from Indianapolis to Formula 1, to
sports cars, and to stock car racing.

Since the earliest part of the twentieth century, Firestone had
been the major player in American racing. The aged company's domination of the Indianapolis 500 had become a centerpiece of its
marketing and sales strategy. Each June, newspapers across the nation
featured a full-page spread touting yet another Firestone victory in the
great race. For decades the Akron-based giant had clear sailing. But in
1957 its major cross-town rival, Goodyear, rose up to challenge Firestone's supremacy. It would take five years for the newcomer to
develop the technology to seriously assault Firestone, but by the mid-
1960s, Goodyear was in play across the board, building first-class race
tires and linking up with major teams in all the significant series.

Because of the early friendship between Henry Ford and Harvey
Firestone, a *de facto* linkage was long established between the two
firms and their racing programs. Newcomer Goodyear had formed an

alliance with Chrysler Corporation, which, like Ford, had broken its nonracing agreement with the Automobile Manufacturers Association, imposed in 1957. While Ford's racing campaign literally spanned the globe, smaller Chrysler concentrated its efforts on the booming worlds of NASCAR and the National Hot Rod Association, where its powerful Hemi V-8s were suited to those forms of competition.

The Firestone and Goodyear racing organizations were operating at full force in 1966. Such powerhouse teams as Richard Petty, Carroll Shelby, and Roger Penske were firmly established in the Goodyear camp, while Parnelli Jones, Holman-Moody, and rising luminary Mario Andretti were loyal to Firestone.

In general, the Fords of the world raced on Firestones, while the Chrysler teams used Goodyears. The funding of such campaigns soared into the uncounted millions. The number, never officially tabulated, probably exceeded over $150 million per year between the four firms—a staggering number in mid-1960s dollars. The expenditures were fragmented in a myriad of budgets: engineering, sales promotion, public relations, marketing, advertising, and travel. Ford, for example, spent tens of millions alone in its 1964–1967 campaign to win the LeMans 24 Hours race, even using charter jets to haul spares between Dearborn and LeMans. At the same time the company unloaded more millions to develop special engines to not only win, but to dominate Indianapolis-type racing. So too for stock car racing, where hefty funds were devoted to displacing Chrysler's all-winning Hemi with a series of exotic, large-displacement pushrod V-8s.

In 1966 Goodyear alone spent $60 million on motor racing, both here and in Europe. A large share of the expenditure went toward tire development—a long and arduous process of trial and error before computer modeling streamlined the whole cycle. Millions were spent in designing and testing prototype tread designs and rubber compounds. Teams of engineers and drivers spent weeks on various race tracks around the nation, running thousands of miles of high-speed testing that was not only exhausting but dangerous. In a little over three months in 1964 and 1965, three top drivers—Jimmy Pardue and Billy Wade for Goodyear and Bobby Marshman for Firestone (in an Indy car)—died in test crashes.

It was a bitter battle between the two tire giants. Espionage was common, and theft of test tires from rival camps happened on more than one occasion. The opposing sides seldom spoke, although the public relations experts from Firestone and Goodyear—Humpy Wheeler and Bill Neely—became good friends offsite. It was, however, a rare situation that contradicted the bitter rift between the two companies.

While Ford and Chrysler fought each other in public, General Motors was a closet competitor, theoretically adhering to the AMA nonracing ban, but quietly spending lavishly to fund the likes of sports car racer-builder Jim Hall, drag racer Mickey Thompson, and stock car genius Smokey Yunick. Again, tens of millions were spent by GM's Chevrolet, Pontiac, Buick, and Oldsmobile Divisions in various forms of motorsports during the 1960s—making it the only period in American motorsport history when almost every major player in the tire and automobile business was engaged.

The battle of the tire giants lasted until 1970, when Firestone, considerably smaller than Goodyear, ran out of steam and money. The monetary muscle of Goodyear was too much, and while Firestone remained involved on a smaller lever, the head-to-head competition across the board ended. So too for Chrysler, which, like Firestone, simply lacked the deep pockets of Ford and General Motors.

Conversely, Ford would carry on through its Cosworth subsidiary to dominate Indianapolis and Formula 1 for several decades, while Goodyear remains in the worldwide motorsports arena to this day. But the battle of the titans during the 1960s will probably never be duplicated in terms of the raw energy and dollars poured into the fray.

It was obvious that the press would be drawn into battle by the various combatants, each with public relations staffers assigned to curry favor with the journalists. Lavish press junkets were common, with expensive gifts handed out to the ink-stained wretches in presumed exchange for favorable coverage. Each company sought a unique angle to attract attention, sometimes pushing the envelope in terms of potential physical harm to the journalists.

Such an incident took place in early 1967, when I was offered a ride at Daytona International Speedway with NASCAR star LeeRoy Yarbrough in his Dodge Charger. It took place during a Firestone tire test for the Jon Thorne team, which had crossed the Chrysler line to run Firestones rather than the usually Goodyears. My good friend H.A. "Humpy" Wheeler was Firestone's racing public relations man. He had promoted stock car races at Gastonia Speedway in North Carolina, then with Firestone during those glory years before joining with entrepreneur Bruton Smith to run the vast Lowe's Motor Speedway complex in Charlotte, North Carolina, where he remains to this day. Wheeler is the key man in the massive Speedway Motorsport Inc., empire and one of the most respected individuals in stock car racing. But in 1967 he was laboring hard to keep Firestone's image polished and its tires in the winner's circle.

It was he who arranged the ride chronicled in the following story I wrote for *Car and Driver*. Today the notion of a writer being permitted to ride around the Daytona Speedway in a stock car at 170 miles an hour without a helmet, driving suit, or even a seat belt, is inconceivable. The levels of liability in the event of a crash would drive a company to the brink of bankruptcy. Yet in those days, such adventures were possible without the specter of trial lawyers looming in the background.

LeeRoy Yarbrough at speed in the Jon Thorne Dodge Charger prior to taking on the author as a high-speed hitchhiker. *Don Hunter*

Yarbrough and the author following their 175-mile tour
of the Daytona International Speedway. *Don Hunter*

What follows is the story of a ride that I will never forget:

Go, LeeRoy!—*Car and Driver*, March 1967

Here it is racing fans, another eyewitness, you-are-there ride in an exotic, high-speed competition car, brought to you in action-packed, three-dimensional prose by one of your thrill-seeking, devil-may-care *C/D* staffers.

Now that you've ridden, with white knuckles and bulging eyes, as it were, in an airfoiled Chaparral, it's time for an entirely new kick; a few 170-mile per hour laps around the Daytona International Speedway with LeeRoy Yarbrough and his lavender and gold Dodge Charger stock car. Before getting under way, it might be a good idea to vicariously buckle up for safety, but in this particular case you'll have to content to huddle on the floor, roughly where the right front seat should be, and brace yourself against the roll cage. You see, there is nothing in the NASCAR rules that requires provisions for passengers, and after a few laps with LeeRoy, the reason for this omission becomes obvious. Nobody in his right mind would ride in there under any circumstances.

Nonetheless, "circumstances" got me in there. There I was, standing around the deserted Daytona pits watching LeeRoy and Buddy Baker test tires, when Firestone's highly respected southern competition boss, Humpy Wheeler, sauntered over and said, "How'd you like to take a couple of laps with LeeRoy?" Responding with a typical lapse of prudence, I said, "Great—let's go!"

The ride was scheduled for the following morning, which gave me time to reflect on my chauffeur, the aforementioned Mr. Yarbrough. After all, you don't want me to climb into a 550-horsepower, 170-mile per hour race car with some near-sighted cretin at the wheel, so I spent a little time reassuring myself about the competence of my driver. I'd met LeeRoy on several occasions, but never had a chance to talk with him at any length. I knew that he's been considered one of NASCAR's bright young stars for several years now but somehow he'd never gotten into any of the first-line factory cars, which made me wonder if somehow he lacked something.

If he had any deficiencies in those formative years, it certainly wasn't driving talent. However, some of the Ford and Chrysler majordomos apparently felt that he was to brusque and cocky—and too much an independent thinker—to fit into a factory racing team.

Yarbrough's cockiness is still there, but it's expressed as self-assurance rather than loud-mouthed bragging. And he has every reason for self-confidence. Operating a Charger with only perfunctory factory aid, he put on a stunning display of driving during the last half of the 1966 Grand National season, setting lap records at a number of superspeedways and winning a major race at Charlotte. "When I'm on a race track, I know my limits," he said at dinner that evening, "I haven't had a car out of shape in a couple of years now, because I know when I get near my limits."

That's what I like to hear LeeRoy, ol' boy, I thought.

The wind at the speedway was blustery the next morning, and Yarbrough contented himself with a few laps in the 178-mile per hour range and some experimentation with hub caps to reduce high-speed turbulence around the wheels. It is creative thinking like this that sets the highly intelligent Yarbrough apart from the rest of the NASCAR pack and qualifies him, in the minds of many southerners, as the next great stock car superstar. He tried the hub caps for a few laps, but gave up because of the wind.

"C'mon, get in," he said. "We'll take a couple of easy laps and I'll show you the line around this place. Actually it's an easy track, once you get the groove down properly. Nowhere near as tough as Darlington, for example," he said as I climbed through the driver's side window and positioned myself on the floor. The floor rug was still there, which made my seat relatively soft, but it was far from hospitable for a passenger.

Your crash helmet! You stupid jerk! I though of my faithful old Bell Magnum in the back of the station wagon, wadded up in my coveralls, and for a moment I thought about retrieving them. Then LeeRoy got in, blocking my exit, and I decided to sit it out like the brave little soldier I am. Yarbrough had his helmet and coveralls on, and began buckling himself into his shoulder harness. "Don't' seem fair, does it?" he said. "Me all strapped in and everything, and you just sittin' there."

"That's OK," I said with unconvincing assurance. "Just don't crash, and I'll be all right."

Yarbrough started the engine and the interior of the car was filled with the guttural blat of the Hemi. He popped the four-speed transmission into first and we bustled out of the pits and toward Turn One. Suddenly LeeRoy jammed on his brakes, jammed the car into reverse and began backing down the track. He rolled along backward for maybe 50 yards and stopped, with his head hanging out of the window. He peered at the track for a few moments and then started up again.

"What was that all about?" I asked.

"Thought I saw a piece of metal on the track," said LeeRoy as he rolled up his window, thereby blotting out some of the noise and all of the wind, "but it wasn't anything but a little chunk of rubber."

Somehow that interlude put me completely at ease. If a race driver is so careful the he scouts the track for foreign matter, he's got to be OK.

As we accelerated toward the first turn, LeeRoy lifted his hands off the wheel and the car veered sharply to the left. "See that? It's the way you have to set up the front end to counteract the banking," he yelled over the rising engine noise.

We ran low the first lap, not even mounting the big banks that rose beside my window like brooding cliffs. I could see the concrete retainer wall clinging to the top of the track, and it seemed impossible that any automobile could negotiate those narrow, precipitous banks without slamming against the scarred, unyielding surface of the wall. On the second lap LeeRoy got on the throttle harder. We slanted up onto the banking of Turn One, and the world tilted sideways 30 degrees, but there were no alarming sensations of any kind. The gentleg-loading shoved me against the roll cage and the noise was nearly deafening, but otherwise it was a piece of cake. There wasn't even any need to hold on, and I sat there self-consciously resting my hands on my knees.

We picked up more speed down the back straight and thundered into Turn Three at something over 100 miles per hour. LeeRoy cut into the lowest of the three grooves and the car began to bounce. He looked at me and signaled the bumpiness, which I acknowledged by nodding my head and smiling—probably a bit maniacally.

Over the nasty bump at the entrance of the pit straight we roared, and the car shot ahead under acceleration. Here we go. I didn't believe that jazz about you taking it easy anyway, LeeRoy.

We were running very fast when we reached Turn One and my first instinct was to grab something. But it wasn't necessary. The car simply banked left like a fighter plane and I wasn't even slightly jostled. Within a few seconds we were on the long back straightaway and I watched the tachometer work its way up to 6,400 rpm. I recalled Jon Thorne, the pleasant young Georgian who owns the Charger, saying that it was equipped with a 3.09 rear axle ratio, and this meant we were turning a substantial number of knots—somewhere near 175 miles per hour.

This time LeeRoy picked the middle groove—and we belted around with me glued into the corner of the car. It seemed like we were

driving straight into the wall. You couldn't see much out of the windshield except black asphalt. This must be one of the dangers of racing
at Daytona; the banks reduce visibility so much that it is difficult for a
driver to see what's happening even a quarter of a mile in front of him.

The ultrastiff suspension rattled up as we sped over the
fourth-turn bump and rocketed down the pit straight with my side of
the car not a foot away from the concrete retaining wall.

By now this was fun. It wasn't anywhere near as hairy as I'd
expected, and I sort of settled back to watch LeeRoy drive. He was
lifting slightly as he entered the banks, although he doesn't on flat-
out runs. A lot of nonsense has been passed around about how
Grand National cars hit 190 miles per hour or so on the straights,
but the fact is that engine speed varies only 200–300 rpm (a few
miles per hour between the turns and the straights at Daytona).

So there we were, motoring around the Daytona International
Speedway at over 170 miles per hour, and it was like a Sunday ride.
On the back straight LeeRoy would look over to see if I had blacked
out or something, and I'd smile and wave my arms around to assure
him I was still functioning. It seemed like a real gas, and I began
snapping some pictures with my faithful old Leica, as we belted into
one of the corners. I lifted the camera to my face—or tried to—and
my arms were lead. The g-loading made it feel as if I were trying to
lift a bag of cement. Last year I rode in the NASA centrifuge at Wil-
low Grove, Pennsylvania, and experienced three Gs under
controlled conditions. This felt like almost as much, and somebody
later said that high speeds at Daytona produce vertical loading of
about two Gs. (It should be stated here—for the sake of journalistic
honesty—that I probably wasn't as cool as I thought during the ride.
The entire roll of film that I shot turned out blank.)

We did a few more laps before one of the Firestone guys signaled LeeRoy to come in. He backed off the throttle and suddenly I

got nervous. Many race drivers will tell you the cool-off lap is the most dangerous, because the driver's concentration lapses, so I really hung on while we rolled through the banks at 150. "Oh, LeeRoy, don't screw up now," I thought.

I tried to look very cool when I clambered out of the car in front of the guys in the pit (especially Humpy, because he's the one who got me in there in the first place). Somebody handed me a slip with the four fastest laps marked on it. Lap one, 169.4 miles per hour; lap two, 171.43 miles per hour; lap three, 171.76 miles per hour; lap four, 172.07 miles per hour.

As it turned out LeeRoy hadn't even been trying. Several days later he mounted some new Firestones, adjusted a couple of experimental spoilers (including one ahead of the windshield that NASCAR refuses to approve for racing) and blasted around the big tri-oval at nearly 185 miles per hour. That was one ride I was perfectly happy to witness from the sidelines.

"That makes you the world's fastest passenger," somebody said. I was about to agree when I thought of the guy who sneaked a ride in Art Arfon's *Green Monster* at over 450 miles per hour, and decided to drop the whole thing. A few guys tried to get me to say how hairy the entire experience was, but it simply wasn't like that. It was smooth and easy—thanks mostly to the beautiful way LeeRoy handled the car, and I could think of two rides that had boosted my blood pressure to considerably higher levels. One was a few laps around Bridgehampton with the late Walt Hansgen in—of all things—a Mercedes-Benz 230 SL, and the other was a trip Steve Smith and I had in a Plymouth Hemi *Golden Commando* funny-car dragster job. I passed out from the initial surge of acceleration and thought the car had tipped over—but that's another story . . ..

So ended my wild day with LeeRoy Yarbrough, but my involvement with Daytona was far from over. One month later, I returned to Daytona to drive my Ray Nichels-built Dodge Dart Trans-Am car in the Daytona 24-Hours. Codriving with friends Chuck Kreuger and Bert Everett, we managed to get the Dodge into the top 10, while running against the full factory teams of Ford and Ferrari. The Dodge, with its 5-liter V-8, was capable of 145–150 miles per hour on the back straight, and I can recall to this day being overtaken in the night by the monster Ferrari P4s and Ford GT MK IVs, their quartz-iodine lights flashing a warning as they wailed past at nearly 200 miles per hour.

Overheating dropped us out of contention in the last hour of the race, but the harrowing, wall-like Daytona banking and the high adventure of a 24-hour endurance race remains one of the high points in my motorsport memories.

LeeRoy Yarbrough will be remembered as one of the potentially great American drivers. His finest season was 1969, when he won the Daytona 500 and was named the best American driver by a panel of experts. He not only excelled in stock cars, but had some solid races in Indianapolis-type open wheelers, entering the Indianapolis 500 eight times, 1965–1971, and finishing three times but not among the leaders (19th, 23rd, and 27th).

Like many of his fellow stock car drivers, including Junior Johnson, Curtis Turner, Bobby Johns, and Cale Yarborough (different spelling, no relation). Yarbrough was attracted to open-wheel racing during the late 1960s and early 1970s, when NASCAR Grand National Racing was embroiled in political turmoil.

Sadly, Yarbrough's life descended toward tragedy following his peak season in 1969, when he won the Daytona 500, the Daytona Firecracker 400, and the Southern 500 at Darlington. A year later he was involved in a serious high-speed crash at the high-banked Texas World Speedway during another tire test. It apparently triggered an undiagnosed brain injury that dogged him for the rest of his days. A year later, on May 8, 1971, he had another testing crash at the Indianapolis Motor Speedway, at the wheel of a Gurney Eagle.

That crash essentially ended his career, although he struggled for another few seasons in minor league competition near his home-town of Jacksonville, Florida. But his behavior became increasingly erratic, caused, some claimed, by a bout of Rocky Mountain spotted fever. Others blamed it on heavy drinking. The probable reason was brain damage caused by the two crashes, which led him to an attempted murder of his mother in 1980. He was judged incompetent to stand trial and admitted to a Florida mental hospital. On December 6, 1984, he suffered a seizure and fell. A day later Lonnie LeeRoy Yarbrough, potentially one of the greatest stock car drivers in history, died, alone and forgotten.

Chapter Eight

DEADLINE FOR DAYTONA, 1968

B ill France had a tiger by the tail. More correctly, several tigers. By 1968 his Grand National (soon to be Winston, then Nextel) Series had become major league by every possible definition. Crowds were up at races everywhere, now staged across the nation from California to Florida. Ford and Chrysler were locked in battle, as were Firestone and Goodyear. Live television coverage was over a decade away, but media attention has accelerated to a point where superstars Richard Petty, Cale Yarborough, and David Pearson rivaled Indy stars A.J. Foyt and Parnelli Jones for headline attention.

Yet there was trouble in paradise. Speeds at Daytona, thanks to artful cheating by virtually everybody to improve aerodynamics, had exceeded to 190 miles per hour—faster than those currently being recorded at the famed track. Bodywork had yet to be androgenized, so the pack-racing seen today on superspeedways was unknown. The cars of 1968 carried stock grillwork, bumpers, and what appeared to be off-the-rack bodywork (an illusion at best). Tires were still bias-ply, and suspension technology was primitive compared to the contemporary computer-modeled setups.

With the stakes getting higher by the year, the battle for supremacy between Ford, Chrysler, Firestone, and Goodyear lost any semblance of sportsmanship. The alignments were basic: The factory-supported Ford and Mercury teams ran on Firestones—based on family linkages dating to the early years of the twentieth century and that remain in play to this day. Chrysler and Goodyear were also hooked up in an alliance, which established two warring camps that would, at 190 miles per hour, shred metal and tempers during the month of February 1968. This is my story of the drama, as produced in the May issue of *Car and Driver*:

Deadline for Daytona

It's all over now; there's nothing but a dim memory of head-splitting sound and bright, blurred automobiles for the 85,000 fans who watched the 10th annual Daytona 500, but the repercussions from this staggering event are still keeping the racing world in turmoil.

The race, indisputably one of the three greatest in the world—along with Indianapolis and LeMans—left practically everybody involved sore at each other. Not that this in itself is an unusual state of affairs, because high stakes invariably prompt short tempers, and it should be noted in the interests of fairness that both LeMans and Indy are also in the middle of nasty disputes about rules-making. Such is not the case at Daytona, where the sides have splintered into a number of dissident, grumbling cliques, rather than dividing into a pair of opposing camps and doing battle over simple issues like turbine power (a la Indy) or sanctioning bodies (a la LeMans).

The disputes at Daytona are as complicated to chart as the ugly skid marks that smear the surface of the awesome, high-banked speedway. Chrysler is mad because it feels it got rooked on the rules, Ford is mad at its sister division, Lincoln-Mercury, for making too much noise over the great performance of its Cyclones; Goodyear and Firestone are sore because each claims the other showed up at Daytona with cheater tires; and the better drivers are a trifle miffed at everybody because they feel they're being exploited on the same sort of short-term basis reserved for kamikaze pilots. All rather confusing, to be sure, but each is relatable to a single element—the man around which the entire world of stock car racing revolved and the single most powerful individual in the entire sport of automobile racing—Bill France.

Although his 10th Daytona 500 was a great success (despite a rainout two days earlier of the 125-mile qualifying races that caused him to return an estimated $175,000 in gate receipts and probably helped to keep his race-day crowd below 100,000), it remains for him to end the dissension and the bickering. He alone can do it, and do it he must if he intends to establish stock car racing as the most important segment of the sport in this nation.

The first problem he must face is safety. Once famous for its relatively low hazard to drivers and fans, Daytona has now become a 190-mile per hour bowling alley, wherein the drivers can apparently run just so far before hitting something. Luckily, in 1968, they only clouted each other and managed to miss the folks in the grandstands.

"You don't drive a car here anymore, you aim it," is the way winner Cale Yarborough described it after qualifying for the pole position at the mind-bending speed of 189.222 miles per hour. "I used to think Daytona was an easy track, but at 190 miles per hour it's more dangerous than Indy."

The man who caught Cale 10 miles from the finish and forced him into second place was LeeRoy Yarborough (unrelated) and he too didn't like the big speeds one bit. "You can maintain the sort of physical strength and mental concentration needed to run 190 miles per hour for only three or four laps before the g loading and nervous strain get to you," he said.

Mario Andretti, who won the 1967 race, observed, "Every time I complete a lap, I wonder if I can do it again."

Sam McQuagg probably summed it up best when he said, "I used to make a mistake once every five laps. At these speeds, I make five mistakes every lap."

Everyone came to Daytona in early February expecting that the maximum speeds would be around 185 miles per hour. Then, through a fluke combination of excellent tire design, whopping horsepower, and highly aerodynamic bodies, a number of brave men began to knock on 190 miles per hour. One quiet morning, when the wind was perfect and the track dry, David Pearson climbed into his gold and blue Ford Torino and lashed around the tri-oval speedway at an incredible 191 miles per hour.

While the super speeds made headlines everywhere and established Daytona as the fastest 2.5-mile closed course in history, they contributed to a rather disappointing race. Despite all the velocity, Cale Yarborough averaged a mere 143.521 miles per hour for the distance—the slowest Daytona 500 to be run since 1960. When he could let loose, he ripped around the track at 184–185 miles per hour, but was slowed by no less than 11 caution flags that inter rupted the pace for 142 miles and 10 pit stops he made to correct a variety of ailments, including overheating and boiling tires. In the opening stages of the event, hardly more than five laps could be completed between crashes. Fortunately only one man—John Sears—was injured (minor cuts) in the messes, but the entire rhythm of the competition was ruined, and the 500 was reduced to a series of frustrating sprints between the action-stopping yellow flags.

Why? Quite simply because there are not 43 cars and drivers in the world capable of zooming around Daytona at 180 miles per hour. At those speeds, cars crumble and drivers make mistakes with such regularity that all semblance of racing is destroyed. Fortu- nately, the tremendous safety provided by today's Grand National stock cars limited the damage to shredded metal and crushed egos, but that was a matter of Divine Providence. Prior to the race there was an atmosphere of impending doom in the pits. "Somebody's going to get it out there today," said one long-time member of the racing fraternity, "I only hope it isn't one of my friends." Another hard-bitten honcho on one of the big factory teams—a man who has been in racing for 30 years—was so worried about the opening laps that he refused to watch what he expected would make the 1964 Indy tragedy look like a lawn party.

Drivers are traditionally oblivious to this sort of pessimism, but they were deeply concerned at Daytona. The best two dozen drivers at Daytona number among the bravest on earth, but it even got to them. "You don't like to bring it up, for fear that you'll seem like a chicken, but once somebody starts talking about it here, you discover that we all feel the same way," said one of the best.

Some of the headliners in the race were involved in crashes— Buddy Baker, Mario Andretti, Jim Hurtubise, Donnie Allison, Bud Moore, James Hylton and Jerry Grant—but all of the major players were affected by the overwhelming difficulty of racing at Daytona. The "Big D" has historically provided magnificent racing because drivers could pass anywhere on the track, sometimes running three abreast through the high-banked turns. A unique feature of Daytona was its fabulous "drafting," a technique whereby two of the three cars tow each other around the tri-oval in a swirl of air. But that tactic practically disappeared with the arrival of the big speeds.

"You drive Daytona like a mile track now," said one driver. "It's a one-groove race track and it's impossible to draft like we used to," he added. "We could race at 175 miles per hour, but at 185 miles per hour, you're lucky to maintain control, much less try to pass anybody or draft in turns," complained another.

And then there were the crowds, those multitudes who sat huddled against the rail with cars zooming past at nearly 200 miles per hour, little more than an arm's reach away. Everyone in the pit area—the men who live by racing—agreed totally that it is perfectly possible (maybe even inevitable) for a car to leap-frog into the grandstands along Daytona's main straightaway. Many of them were aware that Alan Boyd, secretary of transportation and a member of the president's cabinet, was acting as the honorary grand marshal of the race and that if he witnessed a disaster that took the lives of some spectators, it might meant he end of racing in the United States. "If Boyd saw a car sail into those grandstands, he'd just turn away and make one phone call. That'd be it for racing," said one old pro.

Everybody, including the track's management, is aware of the danger. Said a member of the speedway's Board of Directors, "Of course, Bill France realizes the danger, but he's closed his mind to it."

Bill France's attitude is understandable. It was he who single-handedly brought stock car racing from cow-pasture obscurity to the threshold of being the most powerful and lucrative area of American racing. Daytona is the symbol of his success, and he naturally wants to continue his drive to the top until his track completely obscures Indianapolis. To do this, crowds—and prize money—must keep rising and he must gamble that the magic 200 mile per hour lap can be reached. That mark is less than three seconds and an uncertain number of lives away.

While Bill France must wrestle with the rising problems of safety at his track, he is also faced with maintaining a weird balance of power between the major automobile and accessory manufacturers who form the backbone of stock car racing. For two years' Bill France has been bargaining and bartering with these manufacturers to maintain their participation. Being businessmen, they all want an advantage and they all, quite understandably, can't stand to lose. France is therefore confronted with the nightmarish chore of establishing equilibrium between Ford and Chrysler and Firestone and

Goodyear, making sure that no one dominates the sport and that each rival expends a maximum amount of effort (and money) in racing. To do this, Bill France keeps his NASCAR rules flexible (with himself as the final arbiter) and a written regulation in NASCAR is about as reliable as an Egyptian immigration law. This juggling act with the rules has caused some of the most ludicrous disputes in the history of the sport and has kept stock car racing in a constant state of turmoil. Two typical examples relating to the 500 are worthy of note:

In 1964 Chrysler Corporation arrived at Daytona with the famous Hemi and blew the Ford Motor Company clean off the track. It was far from a production engine and Ford complained that the powerplant was illegal. In order to prevent Ford from withdrawing in 1965, France banned the Hemi, which in the meantime had been hastily offered as a passenger car option. Chrysler got sore and quit NASCAR. After a season of sparse crowds, France relented in 1966 and let the Hemi back in, but Ford demanded use of its nonproduction single-overhead cam 427 to counter the potent Mopar threat. France refused and then Ford quit. Finally, in 1967, the automotive Machiavelli worked out a tenuous compromise whereby Ford was permitted the use of two four-barrel carburetors for its old Wedge 427, while the Hemi was limited to a single four-barrel. This ruling, while bringing temporary peace, was uniquely ridiculous because the production version of the Hemi was marketed only with two four-barrels, while the 427 Ford could not be purchased by the public with anything but a single four-barrel setup.

This year Ford arrived at Daytona with "tunnel port" cylinder heads, an improved intake manifold, and a camshaft that gave the old Wedge well over 600 horsepower. In the meantime, the venerable Hemi remained stagnant and the best examples were developing no more than 575 horsepower. To make matters worse, the two four-barrel Ford setup gave considerably better gas mileage, and now Chrysler

has set up an unholy racket about being permitted an extra carburetor. However, if France acquiesces in favor of Chrysler, it is
possible that Ford will quit in protest. On the other hand, Chrysler
is threatening a boycott if he doesn't rule in its favor.

At the same time, Firestone and Goodyear are at each other's
throats in an issue that boils down to the inadequacy of NASCAR's
vague set of rules. All of the hot 190-mile per hour lap speeds at
Daytona came on a special, sparsely treaded Goodyear qualifying
tire that Firestone claimed was illegal. Firestone's representatives
pointed to a rule forbidding "cheater slicks," which promoted a
semantic flap over exactly what NASCAR meant by the term. This
was still unresolved when Firestone showed up with a tire that
Goodyear charged was too wide, according to the rules. Goodyear
was doubly sore when Cale Yarborough used these tires to win the
race, although no official protest was lodged. The NASCAR rule
book says tread width may not exceed 11.69 inches, but also adds
that the final test will be a special profile template through which
the tire must pass. According to Goodyear, their rival's tire measured a thoroughly illegal 12.25 inches, but it would pass—albeit with
a certain amount of pushing and shoving—through the template.
Who's right and who's wrong? Everybody and nobody, probably, but
the rule book is a certain culprit.

One company man put it this way: "The whole system is so
damn vague that everybody has to cheat. You go beyond the rules
and just pray when you get caught that Bill decides to rule in your
favor. Let's face it, man, there isn't a legal car on this race track, and
that includes our products as well as the opposition's."

The cars, to be sure, reached new heights in absurdity. The 20-
old factory-sponsored Fords, Mercurys, Plymouths, and Dodges that
showed up for the race were the wildest collection of streamlined,
slope-nosed, rump-high bogus racers that ever appeared at a "stock"

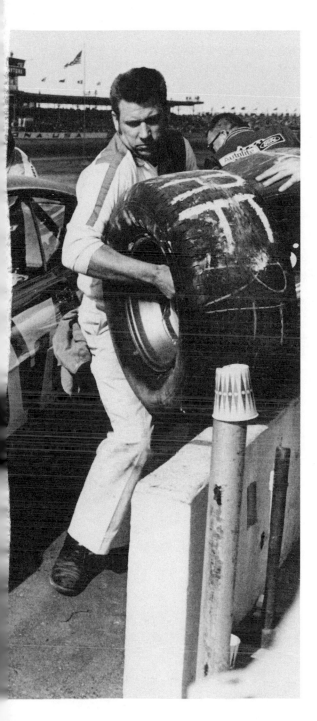

The Holman-Moody crew
makes a tire change on David
Pearson's Ford Torino during
the 1968 Daytona 500.
Hand-operated jacks and stock
lug bolts have been required
in NASCAR competition since
the beginning and place a
priority on physical strength and
dexterity among the pit crew
members. *Don Hunter*

Richard Petty jumps into the fray as he and his crew attempt to repair a loose windshield during the 1968 Daytona 500. Richard lost three laps during the emergency stop. *Don Hunter*

car race. When Mario Andretti blew an engine in practice and crunched his right rear fender, his Mercury Cyclone had to be shipped 500 miles north to Holman-Moody in Charlotte, North Carolina, for two days of custom body repair, leaving the poor-sucker fans to wonder why they just didn't bolt on a new panel from the local Ford garage. When Rookie Butch Hartman parked his relatively stock Charger next to Ray Fox's special, factory-backed Charger in the garage area, Fox put up a great fuss to get it moved. Why? Because Hartman's car stood in bold contrast to exactly how much chopping and slicing had gone into making the factory cars more streamlined. Richard Petty somehow managed to qualify his Plymouth Road Runner 5 miles per hour faster than any other Chrysler product, and a lot of people attributed it to a rough-finish black top that had been painted on the car. But when a magazine photographer managed to sneak a picture of the strange baffling and quasi-belly pans in the Plymouth's engine compartment, one of the Petty crew demanded his film.

And nobody said a whole lot about the fact that this was the second consecutive race that Cale Yarborough won at Daytona with his Mercury Cyclone. Cale won last year's Firecracker 400 in the same car—only then it was called a Ford Fairlane. This year all of the Ford factory cars—excepting LeeRoy Yarbrough's, which was new—were merely '66s or '67s with new sheet metal and called, according to corporate whim, either Ford Torinos or Mercury Cyclones. Because the rules permit this sort of nonsense, the moves were perfectly legal. But, the question remains; what in the hell was Cale driving? The answer is simple: a Ford racing car, a special competition machine, like all the rest in the race, that bears no more relationship to a passenger car than a cross-town bus.

Cale's victory in a "Mercury" brought about another great flap, only this time NASCAR managed to stay clear. Lincoln-Mercury has traditionally been the ugly duckling in Ford corporate affairs, but has recently been exhibiting new spunkiness, much to the distress of the gentlemen in the rival Ford Division. For this year's race L-M hired a group of bright, high-powered young public relations types to trumpet the accomplishments of the men in the Mercurys— namely Cale Yarborough, LeeRoy Yarbrough, Mario Andretti, Tiny Lund, and Jim Hurtubise. They had all the props—jackets, hats, 250,000 bumper stickers, country-and-western bands, and fistfuls of press releases that began making the nation's papers with alarming regularity.

Ford's racing program is supposed to be handled by a single group, with equal emphasis on Ford and Lincoln Mercury. But Ford has traditionally gotten favored treatment. In fact, no Mercurys would have been entered in the race had it not been discovered in test programs that the Cyclone's fastback body was slightly more streamlined and had less frontal area than its twin sister, the Torino. When the Mercurys began to do so well, and the PR types began to tell the world about it, the Ford Division management (which is separate entity to the all-powerful Ford Corporation) began to yell foul and began a last-minute effort to save face. They managed to get a tent show organized, but had to set it up outside the main gate when all the prime infield spots had been taken. In all, the Daytona 500 was a minor disaster for the Ford Division (its best placing was third) all the way to the top floor of the great glass house that is Ford's corporate headquarters in Dearborn.

Although no one can do more than register amusement over the internal flapping at Ford, there is plenty that can be done with NASCAR and the Daytona 500. Like all powerful men, Bill France has many enemies, and you don't have to move more than 4 feet at a major stock car race before someone will tell you that he is a thief and a blackguard who engages in racing purely for personal gain.

This is not true. Surely, he has made mistakes, but the fact remains that he alone has made stock car racing the purest representation of America automobile racing. The racing he has created is enormously colorful and exciting. What's more, it is safe, despite the most aggressive driving styles in racing, and it deserves all of the success that it will enjoy in the years to come.

However, the sport stands at a crossroads. It has now reached a state of importance where Bill France should not have to fiddle with the rules in order to maintain the manufacturers' interest. Stock car racing is major league, and its rules must become inviolate. A set of standards for truly stock automobiles must be established at least a year in advance, and the manufacturers must be forced to live with them. At the same time, the engine displacement should be reduced to 350 ci, with a single carburetor to be sure that the rising speeds do not destroy the sport's great nose-to-nose competition and its fabulous safety record.

Failing adoption of some such restrictive measure, and given the rising danger quotient and the anarchy of the rules, stock car racing's growth, even its existence, are in jeopardy.

Despite this warning—and others—NASCAR could not stop the cheating with body shapes for another 20 years. The mad campaign to create slipperier and more exotic bodies, coupled with ever more powerful engines would not end until 1987. Bill Elliott, driving a Ford, established the official all-time Daytona stock car track record at 210.364 miles per hour during qualifying for the 500. It was then that NASCAR began to revise the rules to control speeds, stabilizing them at roughly that same level run in the late 1960s. Buddy Baker was the first driver to top 200 miles per hour at Daytona in 1970. But following Elliott's record run and his dazzling 212 miles per hour lap at Talladega, also in 1987, NASCAR began to clamp down. In the summer of that year, smaller four-barrel carburetors were mandated, along with restrictor plates for all superspeedways. No 200-mile per hour lap stock car has been turned since then. Although no NASCAR car has ever gotten into the crowd, (as was the concern expressed in this story), Bobby Allison came perilously close during the Winston 500 at Talladega in May 1987. His car sailed into the catch fence protecting the spectators, but slammed back onto the track without reaching the crowd. The race had to be halted three hours while the fence was repaired. This incident prompted Bill France Sr. to decide that speeds had to be radically reduced. Ironically, the ensuing slow-down to current levels has done nothing to affect crowd appeal or attendance. Quite to the contrary, the tight racing of today has led to record attendance and television ratings.

Chapter Nine

THE EARTH MOTHER OF RACING

The day of race queen is long gone. Prerace parades featuring leggy beauties on glitzy floats tossing kisses to the slathering throngs went the way of leather helmets and bias-ply tires, as motor racing moved into a more sophisticated era. But in the 1960s and 1970s a beautiful, busty girl from Dalton, Georgia, rose to the absolute pinnacle of stardom in the sport and, in many ways, remains so to this day.

Linda Vaughn, age unrevealed, has been in the beauty queen business since she was a Miss Georgia runner-up in the Miss America contest. Her first exposure to motor racing came in the early 1960s when she served as Miss Atlanta Raceway. She then arrived on the Grand National circuit as Miss Pure Firebird. A young woman with statuesque beauty and lubricious southern charm, she became a fixture at major stock cars races, rivaling many of the drivers in pure crowd appeal.

Rumors surged through the sport that she was the lover of superstar Fireball Roberts, who died in July 1964 following a terrible May 24 crash at Charlotte, North Carolina. Then came World Champion and Indianapolis winner Jimmy Clark, who lost his life in 1968.

By then Linda had hooked up with George Hurst, the brilliant but star-crossed designer and manufacturer of the famed Hurst shifting mechanism for domestic four-speed transmissions. After becoming the third—and most famous—Miss Hurst Golden Shifter, Linda Vaughn embarked on a lifetime of promotional tours, becoming a star attraction at auto shows, trade shows, conventions, and motor racing event.

The following story was written for *Car and Driver* after a few weeks with the dazzling lady. It outlined the personality of a major presence in motorsports, who remains on center stage to this day.

Shortly before this story was written, I attended Linda's wedding to drag racer Billy Tidwell. It seemed a hastily arranged mismatch and my ensuing story implied trouble ahead for the pair. Linda was furious and our friendship soured for a while—until the marriage broke up after a short time. While I now only see her occasionally at various shows and races. Our friendship has been repaired while she carries on as the best-known female in the history of motor racing.

Linda—*Car and Driver*, June 1970

"Ah love 'em all, just like my little brothers and sisters."

The Bakersfield drag races are run on an abandoned military airfield planted in the middle of a treeless, haze-shrouded basin. It is flat and featureless from horizon to horizon, save for low rows of bleachers that border the track and a rickety orange control tower painted with a sign that says, "Kern County Racing Association." The numbing thunder of the machines is silenced. Practice and qualifying are over, and the elimination rounds are about to commence. The national anthem is partially digested by the aged public address system.

Then it appears at the far end of the track, shimmering and unworldly against a gray backdrop of smog. It is a white convertible with a great pole probing out of its trunk lid—a phallus 10 feet tall— a giant shift lever draped with this fantastic, silver-haired, pneumatic woman. My God, its Linda! "And here she is, ladies and gentleman, the queen of racing, the lovely Linda Vaughn, Miss Hurst Golden Shifter!""Linda, baby. Up here!""Lookit that hair.""Unreal!" "Man, oh man, what boobs!" "Linda, baby, you got a good thing going!" "Bow, Linda, Bow!"

Linda Vaughn faces the crowd and sweeps into an exaggerated bow. Suddenly there is a cleavage that looks like somebody split that glowing skin with an axe. Wolf whistles. Shouts. Arms waving. Hands clapping. Binoculars are focused. Brownie cameras cock and fire. The few women present watch in wooden silence. The lean, golden-sheathed body snaps upright and the long-sharp-chinned face breaks into a wide, innocent grin. An arm flutters, the great bosoms turn in a gallant profile, the massive, sensuous streams of hair sway in the breeze and the voice shouts, in shrill, southern little-girl tones, "Hi y'all!"

Then Miss Linda Vaughn, Miss Hurst Golden Shifter, former Miss Pure Firebird, former Miss Atlanta raceway, former Miss Georgia runner-up, the queen of auto racing, the earth mother of all racers, big sister to brave boy-men, the sweet, indomitable Little Annie Fannie of the Speedways, life and fertility symbol of motorsport, has passed by.

The racing is over. The sun is falling and clusters of men and their women with beehive hair are standing around inert cars. Bored kids are stomping plastic cups under the bleachers, minibikes buzz. People squint against the punishment of blowing grit. Accessory company representatives in miracle-fiber warm-up jackets paste decals on the winning cars, and a platoon of photographers record the presentation of enormous, polished-wood trophies to the victors. In the middle is Linda, resplendent, bright-eyed, loquacious, unmarked by the hours of rubbing and hugging that she has carried on with a thousand, hungry, fantasy-crazed fans. Autographs, kisses, poses for Instamatics and Polaroid Swingers, enough "Hi y'alls" to rupture a Georgia peach, and miles and miles of smiles.

In a small trailer behind the timing tower another woman is watching the performance. She is Caroline Williams, the wife of Jack Williams, a veteran drag racer who promotes the Bakersfield event. Caroline Williams is no bush leaguer. An ex-Playboy Bunny in miniskirt and frosted hair, she has assisted Linda with her costume changes throughout the day, thereby becoming a true witness to the legend of the Vaughn physical presence. She leans easily against the trailer door, smiles laconically, and says, "One thing about Linda, she sure can make you feel like a boy."

The Lions Drag Strip in Long Beach, California, is dark, and sea air makes the pit area damp and chill. It is clogged with racing cars, painted like lace curtains, pickup trucks with camper bodies, delivery vans, raked street jobs with mag wheels, and that awful, seismic, mantle-ripping drum-ruffle sound of fuel-burning, super-charged V-8 engines. Linda is there, swirling through the pits, sliding easily into open arms, snuggling against tingling torsos, joking, waving, chattering in a hundred brief encounters. Hovering nearby is a young man in a wheelchair—a bashful youth whose awkwardly canted legs indicate that his occupancy in the chair had been long and difficult. He watches her with the awe and simple affection reserved for untouchables, for idols, for goddesses. Whenever she appears at Lions, he is there, to watch and to roll along behind at a respectable distance. Linda goes to him as she goes to the rest, grasping his hand and carrying on a brief, autonomic conversation laden with innocent pleasantries. The boy is pleased, and suddenly the mentality of "fandom" and the relationship of glamour to loneliness gains meaning.

Linda gets hundreds of letters a week. Dozens include earnest proposals of marriage and tokens of affection. Valentine's Day brings boxes of candy and syrupy expressions of love. To most of them she is little more than a plastic doll life symbol mounted on the back of a convertible. To others she exists as a living, breathing, talking human being, and when all the heated loins and pulsating glands have cooled, she remains for them not the embodiment of sexual fantasy, but a lusty, big sister. "Linda has a way of letting guys down easy," says a friend. "They get all pumped up when they see her, and you'd think she'd have trouble with a lot of them, but she's so sweet and genuinely friendly that nobody can get sore at the way she says no."

Others recall an incident at Indianapolis several years ago when a drunken, grease-stained mechanic broke into a cocktail party Linda was attending and dressed in a flowing formal. The mechanic elbowed his way through the crowd and asked Linda to dance; she accepted instantly. The dance completed and her partner's ardor dampened, if not satisfied, he staggered away and the party resumed. "Linda handles things like that better then any woman I've ever met," said a friend who witnessed the incident. "If she'd turned up her nose at the boy, there would have been a nasty scene, but she has an instinctive sense about how to handle men and their egos."

Linda, and her men. Aside from the few serious involvements in her 26 years and the scattered adventures of her early career in southern stock car racing, her relationship with the racing community is surprisingly asexual. "Everybody thinks I'm in the sack with everybody else," she says, "but the fact is, I really consider the guys in racing my friends. In a sort of general sense I'm married to all of them, but only in the way that they relate to the sport. When I started out in Atlanta, the glamour of racing was pretty big thing to a little ol' country girl from Dalton, Georgia, and I sort of went off the deep end. But I'm older and smarter now, and my personal life is

And takes naught but from itself.

Love possesses not

Nor would it be possessed.

For love is sufficient unto love.'

"That really got to me. Here was all this money, and I was still as lonely as before. The next morning I got on the airplane for home. Then I gave him back that great, big beautiful rock. It damn near broke my heart.

"For me, racing is everything."

It is 4:20 in the morning and the Delta Airlines passenger lounge at the Los Angeles International Airport is desolate and still. Rumpled forms are sprawled on the green vinyl couches and a few uniformed agents slump at their desks. In the corner a pair of swarthy janitors with 1954 grease-ball hair stop their mopping to watch the tall blonde sweep into the room. She is wearing a blue denim slack suit that covers a great deal of her spectacular figure, but the foliage of platinum hair gives her 5-foot, 6-inch body a larger-than-life aspect that sometimes makes her looks 11 feet tall.

She spots the hunch-shouldered form of a tired man and strides to him. A hug. Chatter. Then silence. The moment is serious. The man is Tommy Lemmons, frontline mechanic for the great Don Garlits. Hours earlier, his boss' car had exploded in half at the Lions Drag Strip, and now Garlits lies in the intensive care unit of the Pacific hospital with part of his right foot shorn off and his left leg broken.

Lemmons is man with soul, and he is heartened by the company. Before Linda's arrival it was his job to alone greet Garlits' wife, Pat, who is rushing through the night from Tampa to be at the side of her wounded husband. These are hard moments in racing, when legend says that the insiders—those who understand the hurt—bunch together in a protective cover over the stricken. Linda had heard about the crash at Bakersfield, 150 miles to the north and

my very own. Forget all the fantasies, and you'd be surprised how really cool I am."

They remembered her with Fireball. It was a legendary combination. Fireball Roberts, the fastest, smartest stock car driver of the early 1960s, and the nubile Linda, first the "Queen" of the Atlanta Raceway, the Miss Pure Firebird—wherein she legged the first of several thousand miles of touring race tracks perched on a performance totem (in this particular case, a scarlet, winged bird, symbol of Pure Firebird gasoline.) "He used to call me 'Bird,' and he taught me a whole lot about life," she says as she regally raises her chin in unconscious gesture of sadness and nostalgia. Although Roberts was married throughout his friendship with Linda and at the time of his tragic death in 1964, her devotion to him is obvious. She says she loved him, but for her love is an oft-used euphemism for many subtle gradations of affection, more often relating to family-figures than to paramours. She says she loved Jimmy too, meaning the late Jim Clark, who saw Linda a great deal more than the racing fraternity realized before his fatal crash in 1968. "He had so much class—he was such a gentleman," she says in that sharp voice of hers, full of cornpone county Georgia thickness, but strangely punctuated by precise articulation. If shorn of her accent, she would have extraordinary elocution.

"We used to sit around in the motel room and talk and I'd rub his back. It was a beautiful thing, and one of the proudest things I could every have done in my life would have been to have borne one of Jimmy Clark's children. He was a great man. Most race driver are lousy lovers. They are too wrapped up themselves, too impatient. But he was different. I can remember the day he died. I was working the New York Automobile Show and a call came while I was on the stand. It was Booper calling from Atlanta ("Booper" is Linda's close friend, Betty Drye, shapely North Caroline who is something of a legend in

The incredible Linda Vaughn with the author at Irwindale, California. *Car and Driver archive*

her own right.) I said, 'Who?' and she answered, 'Jimmy,' I left the show right away and went to my hotel room and called her back. We bawled on the phone for an hour.

"Most race drivers would make terrible husbands, because of their ego problems. But I would have married Jimmy. He has so much class.

"Sometimes I get so lonely I could bawl my damn eyes out."

Linda Vaughn was engaged to be married once. Her suitor was a balding, 50ish, ex-Air Force general with powerful connections with the military industrial establishment. He had millions, and he seemed prepared to spend them on his wife-to-be. Linda appeared at the races wearing a diamond ring that would make even Liz and Dick blink. Its center stone was 10 carats, surrounding by a grouping of 1-carat subordinates. It cost the earth. He owned executive jets, and suddenly her primary mode of transport was Saberliners and Lears.

"For a while I thought it was the real thing. Then he started to call up at odd times, just trying to catch me cheatin' on him. Then more and more, it seemed like I was a big-busted blonde that he could show off. I finally talked him into a trip to Europe—just the two of us, no business, no friends—to really see if we worked together. It was going to be a dream trip; we were going to travel by Lear, you know, first class all the way. Then the first minute we get to our hotel in Paris, surrounded by all this romance, the rat gets on the telephone to make a trans-Atlantic call!

"It all ended in this Swiss chateau one night when he had gone off on another of his business things. I was alone and it was raining and I felt terrible. I began reading Rod McKuen—he's my favorite—and Kahlil Gibran's "The Prophet," and I read a passage that said,

'Love gives naught but itself

had hurried to help. Of the thousands of people in Southern California who tell you they are bosom buddies of "Big Daddy," only Vaughn had stayed up all night in order to do what she could.

"These days you gotta be an artist to be a chick."

It's never far away, the little leather bag with all the cosmetics stuff; the brushes and paint and the powder puffs and mascara, and the mirror that she uses to eye herself a hundred times a day. Riding in the back seat of a friend's Eldorado ("love those Eldos"), passing a mirror in a hotel lobby, catching a reflection in a store window, it's the same; a detached examination of appearance—to tug a wrinkle to form the dress, to finger curl a strain of hair, to blend the makeup shading on a cheekbone—constant tampering with the external self. Then the bag. Out comes a comb or an eyebrow pencil or another application of Jasmine cologne. Inside the bag is a great deal of psychic protection against the world. Don't count the .25 caliber Beretta Jetfire automomatic that sometimes lurks in there, because a woman with a visibility quotient like hers can attract degenerates of both sexes. But the cosmetics are meaningful, as is the bulging, grayed wallet full of family pictures—nieces, nephews, brothers, sisters, step-brothers, cousins. There is a mother, a youthful woman in a ragged Walgreen color photo, leaning against the top of a pink and black Ford hardtop. "My mamma is the greatest," she says. "We've always been very close. I go home in Dalton to see her as much as I can, and keep her up to date on all the things that are happening to me. She was a little mad at me when I wouldn't marry the general, but you've got to understand that life has been pretty hard for my mamma, raising all of us kids like she did. She could just see all that money slippin' away My daddy, he's a pretty wild ol' boy and they've been divorced a long time now. Last time I saw him, he was drivin' around a big ol' Eldo with a chick younger than me sitting beside him."

There is a picture of herself, taken during a brief vacation in Hawaii with "My boy"—a reticent, introspective, hard-running race driver for whom she harbors great affection. She is standing loosely in front of a low, vanilla-colored hotel on the Island of Maui. Her hair is unteased and lies flat against her head. She is wearing slacks and a sweater and a pair of sneakers. Her face is without makeup. She looks childlike, innocent, maybe 16 years old.

Then she snaps the wallet shut and buries it inside the bag. Before she locks the clasp, the mirror comes out for a quick perusal. Everything is in order.

"I've been doing this for eight years. Two more and it's all over."

Nobody has ever stopped to figure out why automobile racing, of all the major sports, has a queen symbol like Linda Vaughn, but the fact remains that she is the best-known female ever to snuggle up to an automobile or to the man who drives it. She is a good broad. Somehow through all the madness and sadness, the hustlers and the phony lovers, she has managed to keep smiling, to keep looking forward to tomorrow and another ride around another racetrack on the trunk of the convertible. She is unsinkable. In the course of her work with Hurst, she visits numerous military hospitals and plays big sister to thousands of smashed young men from Vietnam. She plows cheerily through the wards and solariums, a smile glued to her face. Then she flees to a car and cries uncontrollably.

She has been romanced by some of the biggest names in sports and entertainment, married and unmarried. One of America's most famous racing personalities asked her to marry him. Joe Namath squired her briefly, until she bailed out on him in a nightclub. The father of one of the world's international racing stars offered her big money and a life of leisure if she would become his mistress. She declined.

"Two more years and that's it," she says. "My association with Hurst, especially with George and his wife, and Jack Duffy (the balding, aggressive, extremely capable Hurst PR boss) whom I respect more than anyone in this business, will stay close, I hope. But I want to develop a career based on advertising and public relations. My idol is Mary Wells, and I figure if she can do it, I can do it."

And why the hell not?

Chapter Ten

THE GRADUATES

B y the mid-1960s, Curtis Turner had been welcomed back into the NASCAR tent after his "life-time" banishment for trying to organize the drivers into the Teamsters Union. While in his 40s, he had lost none of his legendary skills, either as a driver or as a party animal. I had become good friends with him over the years and quickly accepted an invitation to attend his new race drivers' school in Charlotte, North Carolina, with two major celebrities of the day. James Garner was at the time one of the hottest male stars in Hollywood and an acknowledged racing enthusiast. He had starred in John Frankenheimer's epic *Grand Prix* (after Steve McQueen had turned down the role) and was a regular in Southern California racing circles. Dick Smothers was, with brother Tommy, starred in *The Smothers Brothers Comedy Hour* on CBS. The former folk singer and straight man for his zany brother was a serious race driver with considerable potential.

The driving school was sponsored by Goodyear and was part of a fierce struggle with cross-town rival Firestone for dominance in America motorsport. The two were spending tens of tens of millions annually in an effort with win in all forms of racing. They would remain locked in combat until Firestone flinched in the middle 1970s, its bottom line suffering from the billowing expenditures needed for research and development, plus team contracts, while the passenger tire business faltered.

The Curtis Turner trip was one of many public relations efforts initiated by Goodyear to keep its brand in the news. I was one of a handful of journalists invited along to enter the school and to write the following story for *Car and Driver* in the June 1968 issue—a piece that did little to advance the cause of Goodyear in the big-time world of automobile racing.

Dick Smothers and Jim Garner Matriculate Under Curtis Turner

The cast of this highly improbable scenario numbers many hundreds, but the leads are played by three pretty well-known individuals. First you've got Curtis Turner, better known as "Pops"— the wildest stock car driver who ever T-boned some good ol' boy into the third row seats; James Garner, an authentic movie star and back-yonder television cowboy, genuine car nut who got hipped on racing during his starring role in *Grand Prix*; and Dick Smothers (the smart one), the ex-Purple Onion folk singer who is now coproprietor of one of TV's biggest variety shows and a real racer of considerable talent.

The story line is about how these two celebs go south to Charlotte, North Carolina, and take some lessons in Pops' high-performance driving school. Now there isn't much plot except some old NASCAR-type drinking and hell-raising, a lot of crashing and banging around a dirt track and learning how to do bootleg turns with a bunch of "Chivalays" that refuse to die, and stuff like that. It was great fun, I guarantee, because everything that Curtis Turner does is fun, including landing an Aero Commander on the main street of Easely, South Carolina, on a Sunday morning and doing just fine taking off again until some little o' lady in a Falcon turned out of a side street in front of him.

Of course she had the light with her, but that's hardly enough reason to block the way of a 200-mile per hour airplane fixin' to take off, is it?

But that's another story, and I don't want to stray too far from this business of Smothers and Garner at the driving school, and how they showed a lot of the good ol' boys who came out to watch that they weren't a pair of flaky actor-types, but were real guys who could handle Pops' Chivalays as well as anybody.

The details for the affair were set up by a bunch of neat guys from Goodyear, headed by the company's racing boss, Larry Truesdale. After a weekend of lying around Pinehurst and being treated real right by a bunch of folks at the Rockingham Speedway, Paul Goldsmith showed up with a Cessna Four-Eleven, and Truesdale, Garner, Smothers and I flew up to Charlotte. About the time we talked Goldsmith out of showing us how easy it is to do slow rolls in a Four-Eleven, we landed at Charlotte, and Dick Ralstin, Goodyear's racing PR man, appeared with a pair of Avises and we made it directly toward the Charlotte Motor Speedway.

Curtis Turner, who was the motivating force behind the speedway before he got aced out in a series of financial disasters, currently rents a portion of the track's 400-odd acres for his school. The operation, formally called the International School of Safe High Performance Driving, is sort of a two-phase deal, designed on the one hand for tyro race drivers, and on the other for law enforcement officers, salesmen, and, presumably, the occasional whiskey hauler, who all want to sharpen their highway driving techniques. The school lasts a week and includes classroom sessions, driving on both dirt and macadam surfaces, Link Trainer-type testing and a series of impromptu races involving everybody—students, instructors, and overeager spectators.

Pops was waiting for us at the track entrance, looking big as a house. He was decked out in a pair of white slacks, a flat-top cowboy hat pulled down over his eyes, and he carried a clipboard. A lot of other guys were there too, including a local reporter who kept following Garner around telling him how much he used to like him in *Maverick*—which brings up a point. If you should ever run into Garner, don't bother telling him about how much you liked him in *Maverick*, because he isn't particularly proud of that interlude in his career and doesn't get a terribly big hoot about recalling those good old days, which weren't much good anyway.

We stood around talking about how George Washington once slept in the house that now serves as the administration building of the Charlotte Motor Speedway, and then motored over to an expanse of red clay that serves as the training grounds for Pops' school. A half-dozen regularly enrolled students showed up, plus the instructors—a friendly bunch of area stock car drivers who were very polite and insisted on calling everybody "Mr." just as if they were teaching at Duke or Wake Forest.

Now I'm not kidding when I tell you Smothers is a real racer. He drives his Brabham Formula B car in West Coast SCCA events and does very well, they say, despite the fact that it's his first year He just bought a Gurney-Eagle Formula A car for the new SCCA pro series, and his buddy, Dr. Lou Sell, will drive it—that is until Dick gets a little more experience and takes a crack at it himself. Both he and Garner know a great deal about the sport—maybe 50 times as much as your average local car buff, and a lot of time was spent with each of them comparing notes on their respective racing efforts. Garner isn't driving himself, mainly because he feels too many guys associated with his production company depend on him whole and in good shape. But he really came on during the filming of *Grand Prix* and won the respect of the European racing community for his genuine ability behind the wheel. Now he's operating the American International Racers and following this business in Charlotte, he showed up at Sebring and watched Scooter Patrick lead the opening stages of the race and set the fastest lap in one of his Lola Mark III coupes.

Garner dug around in his bag and produced the red and blue striped helmet that he had worn in *Grand Prix*, while it took Smothers a bit more time to get ready for action. First it was a pair of fireproof coveralls, then a set of driving gloves, then a helmet that looked like maybe Pablo Picasso had charged him $11,000 to decorate. It was a lavish silver and blue pattern, sort of like an abstract tire print, and "Dick" was scrolled across the visor.

It was time to begin class, and the first lesson involved a simple reverse spin. Now this is a basic bootleg turn, in which you motor down the dirt strip lined with rubber cones, throw the wheel over, stab the brakes, and after the car hunkers over on its outside wheels and teeters precariously for a few moments, it spins around and ends up facing the direction it came from. The instructors brought out a pack of well-crunched 1968 Chevys—a couple of Camaros, two Chevelles, and an immense Impala—and everyone set to work. To make things easier, the front brakes had been unhooked (although you can do the same thing merely by using the parking brake, should you want to try it in your own car, on your very own street) and after a few times everybody was spinning around in pretty decent fashion. Then Pops rode up on a 50-cc Honda and a few of the good ol' boys retired to a station wagon to watch the action. "We're spinnin' 'em now in a 50-foot lane, but before the school is over, everybody will be able to spin in 24 feet," Pops announced. "After all, a reg'lar highway ain't but 24 feet wide, and if the cops was chasin' you or something, you'd have to be able to spin out in that width."

Pops wasn't kidding about the cops, because he was maybe the best liquor hauling driver in the South in the 1940s. Somebody got out a bottle of Canadian Club and began passing it around and we all sat there, slugging shooters of C.C. and Coke chasers, and listening to Pops tell how to spin a flatbed truck loaded with liquor in the middle of a two-lane bridge at 80 miles per hour.

The next lesson was a reverse spin, where you get running backward about 40 miles per hour and then crank the wheel over and, hot damn, next thing you know, you're going back the way you came. It wasn't too hard to learn, once you got over the urge to punch the brakes. Then, when Larry Truesdale was looping around, a tire blew. Everybody laughed a lot, because Goodyear supplies the tires for Pops' school, but it should be mentioned that both the tires and the cars used in the school are over-the-counter stock. The tires, which get flogged and ripped around like you wouldn't believe, are amazingly durable. And so are those old Chivalays. Equipped with the regular heavy-duty suspension, they are driven silly from morning to night, with almost unbearable loads placed on their engines, transmissions, and suspensions. In fact, one of the cars had been pulled out of class to engage in a little intramural dicing in the first NASCAR GT race at Rockingham the week before. A 396 Chevelle, it was the only one of the fleet equipped with a roll bar, and had been pressed into service when race day dawned with a paucity of machinery in the pits. Miraculously, it had finished the 250-miler with no ill effects. Pops claims they've had no serious failures since the school opened last summer, and maintenance involves only about $150 in parts a month. However, when a student the instructors had nicknamed "Snowflake" got through with one of the Chevelles, Pops' maintenance bill jumped considerably. But I'm getting ahead of my story.

We ran a few more reverse spins, and Garner and Smothers got interviewed by a local TV station, and were standing around talking with the ol' boys, who were talking to them because they are regular guys, and then Pops said it was time for a little work on the track. The 1 1/2-mile Charlotte Motor Speedway loomed in the background, but it wasn't time for us to try that one—yet. Pops was talking about a roughed out, rutted oval that rambled over the crest of a hill near the field where we'd been spinning. Down at the far end, where the third and fourth turns were obscured by a knoll, stood a cluster of trees. Somebody explained that it was graveyard—a burial ground for the slaves who worked the plantation that entertained Washington and that sort of thing—and a lot of guys started mumbling about how it was the only race track they knew of the had a cemetery in the infield.

It had been raining in Charlotte, and the track looked like those roads you see in World War I pictures of springtime troop movements toward Verdun. Pops said he better check the track and got into one of the Camaros, while one of his instructors, a friendly, brush-cut local champion named Stick Eliott got into another. The good ol' boys began chuckling in anticipation, because Stick is a pretty fair country race driver, and they knew he'll take a crack at blowing off ol' Pops, especially with all the movie stars around and everything.

They could barely make headway through the mud for the first couple of laps but then Pops and Stick began to wear a couple of ruts into the track and they upped their speed. Down over the hill we could hear them punch the throttles, coming out of Turn Three and, son-of-a-gun, here they came down the chute past us, making maybe 70 miles per hour. Then they tossed those Camaros sideways and broadslided through the first turn, flinging clots of Carolina clay the size of baseballs at the delighted crowd. Pops had a slight lead, but ol' Stick was trying his damndest to get by. On the next lap they busted past us even faster, and Stick shoved the nose of his Camaro practically into Pops' left elbow. "Hot damn, them ol' boys are really racing," somebody hollered.

"You just wait. Pops'll fix ol' Stick, " another answered. Sure enough, the pair of them busted over the crest of the hill with the cemetery in the background and Pops wailed into Turn One so fast it looked like he was going to end up in Concord—which is 6 miles down the road. Stick tried it too, but the Camaro did a tight snap-spin and a great roar went up from the assembly. "I told you, Pops led ol' Stick down the garden path—does it every damn time. No shit, ain't nobody ever drives the dirt like Pops."

After that little exhibition, nobody there was about to dispute that statement, and Garner was going around with a big smile on his face saying, "No sir! Not me. No way you're going to get me to do that!" But it wasn't three minutes before he was in one of the Chivalalys busting around out there as quick as anybody. Smothers kept saying things like, "Man, that looks like a groovy thing to do," and he meant it. As soon as he got a chance he jumped in a car and was going like crazy.

The smarties will tell you that dirt track racing is a primitive thing, but they ought to try it once before they run their mouths. It's very tricky, and we found that out the first time we started to go around a corner. The trick is not in entering—where you can fling a car sideways and just punch the throttle to keep the tail hung out—but exiting a turn onto the straightaway. Pretty soon we were spinning out like a pack of bumper cars and the Chivalays began to overheat and every once in a while somebody would throw a tire. But Pops would just let the engines cool down for a minute, or change the rubber, and send the cars right back out.

About the time the track was getting worn in a bit and we were all getting a little sharper—which means we could make maybe three laps without spinning into the drainage ditch that bordered the backstretch—Paul Goldsmith arrived. This set a lot of the good ol' boys to reminiscing about all the great races Paul and Pops

Curtis Turner with the author at Atlanta. Both appear to be in reasonably good condition despite an all-night party at the legendary driver's Charlotte, North Carolina, home the night before. Richard Petty's Plymouth is parked in the background. *Car and Driver archives*

Curtis Turner ends his scorching drive in the 1967 Daytona 500. Driving the controversial Smokey Yunick Chevelle, Curtis won the pole at a record breaking 180.831 miles per hour—the first time 180 miles per hour had been surpassed at Daytona. He dominated the race until his engine failed 100 miles from the finish. *Car and Driver archive*

used to have on the dirt in the old days, and the conversation made Paul so sentimental that he thought he'd try a few laps for old time's sake. Now the car he brought along was a big green Chrysler 300 four-door—not exactly your perfect dirt track machine—but Paul put three other guys on board and the next thing he was out there flinging that monster around like a damn ol' modified. Well almost. You see, Garner was racing him in a Camaro, and Paul had to try pretty hard to keep up. Finally a tire popped off the rim and the Chrysler spun out and Paul had to retire, but he had a helluva time while he was running.

That was about it for the first day of class, and we all adjourned back to the Howard Johnson Motel, where some of the guys took a sauna and the rest of us settled for a shower and a few shooters. Joe Whitlock was staying there, mainly because he was doing a test on a couple of Fords and he and Big John and I sat around his room telling stories about ol' Duzie, who is the biggest— how do you say it?—prophylactic manufacturer in North Carolina and is a very funny man to boot. All of this stuff was a sort of warm-up for one of Pops' famous parties, which he was laying on over at 4000 Freedom Drive. Noah's rain had started by the time we got there, but that hadn't kept maybe half the city of Charlotte (the right half, believe me) from being on hand. Garner and Smothers swung right into the action and everybody stood around drinking shooters and doing, well you know, the things you do at a Curtis Turner party. That is not to say anybody misbehaved, because about the only wild thing that happened was when ol' Domer decided to start tackling some baby dolls. He'd line up on the other side of the bar room and charge into some poor chick like he was Ray Nitschke or somebody. Domer decked quite a few baby dolls that way, and then somebody took off his pants and recited a version of the "Night Before Christmas" that nobody had ever heard before, and a lot of people got tuned "about right" as Pops would say, and then we all went home. After all, we had class in the morning.

It was gloomy and cold the next morning, and the massive Charlotte Motor Speedway looked gray and forbidding when we arrived on the long back straightaway for more lessons on spin-outs. Off in the infield, I could see the trailer that housed 15 tons of high explosives that was being used to clear away a mound of granite. I figured sooner or later one of the students was going to ram into that thing and we'd probably get out of the class early— very early.

We did some spins on the pavement, and then they moved the cones into 24 feet and we all got so we could spin frontward and backward without knocking any over. Smothers discovered that somebody's Avi Barracuda would spin like a demon and we all made a couple of passes in that and sure enough, it worked just fine. You could hardly feel the flat spots in the tires when we got through. Then class was over and ol' Alan Hill loaned Pops his Fleetwood Caddie and Pops did a reverse spin just as perfect as you please. Oh, the tires smoked more than the Chivalays, but Pops never touched a pylon, and that was most important.

The sun came out in the afternoon and we all went over on the front straightaway to work with a single slalom course that you were supposed to take at about 70 miles per hour. Pops said you could get through it at 90 miles per hour, but you'd spin out at the end, so 85 miles per hour was about the best speed, but he wanted us to all start at about 70 miles per hour at first.

One of the first guys to try was named Snowflake, a kid from Alaska who wanted to be a race driver. He said he'd only driven 4,000 miles in his life, and claimed that the nearest paved road was 500 miles from his house. He wasn't taking to the course too quickly, so the instructors told him to run the first few passes through the slalom kind of easily. But Snowflake was one of those guys who likes to press the button, no matter what, and sure enough, he came wailing though there at about 75 miles per hour and lost it on the infield grass. We all stood there for what seemed like five minutes while Snowflake's Chevelle went spinning across the grass toward the infield, and all I could think of was, Good God, there goes the dynamite. But then the pit wall—which is steel— loomed and Snowflake hit it a mighty whack right in the tail end. Everybody ran over, and ol' Snowflake climbed out and said he was OK, so the instructors figured the car wasn't hurt too bad and they let him try again.

Everybody was standing back a little bit when Snowflake came through a second time, and sure enough, he was going faster than his first pass. "There he goes again," somebody yelled, and we all stood there and watched while Snowflake spun, at maybe 80 miles per hour, and headed for the outside wall. This time it didn't look so funny—and when he hit, a terrible report rumbled across the speedway and suddenly the whole front end of the Chevelle was all kinked and mis-shapen. It bounced away from the wall and skidded down the track with ol' Snowflake slumped over the wheel. But by the time the first guys got to him, he had shaken off his daze and was walking around his busted racer. It was a mess, both the front and back were crunched beyond repair, and Pops said it was ready for the junk heap.

While Snowflake stood around acting sheepish, everybody decided that was the end of class for the day and it was back to the motel for more shooters and saunas. Just before we left, a bunch of high school kids busted through the gates and charged Smothers and Garner for autographs. With them was our bellhop from the motel. He was playing hookey from school to take in the action at the track, and spotted his homeroom teacher in that gang of kids. Oh well, that's the price you pay for hanging around with movie stars.

We had dinner that night in a joint in Charlotte, and Smothers and Garner were talking racing with Goldsmith—who was sitting between them—when this guy came up from another table, grabbed Garner's hand and must have blown his cool in the presence of greatness, because he blurted out, "Jim, you are my greatest fan." Then he turned to Goldsmith and said, "And Dick, me and the little woman always watch your show too." That'll teach Smothers to wear his glasses in public.

It was kind of the same thing again that night, what with Pops throwing another party, with Whitlock getting drunk along with about 300 other guys. Both Smothers and Garner seemed to be having a genuinely good time, mainly because everybody was treating them like just a couple of ol' boys, except for the occasional dude whose daughter would die of heartbreak unless she got their autographs for themselves but they are terribly thoughtful about making sure their kids get the right signatures.

There were more spinout lessons the third day, plus some classroom business that brought back memories of a Saturday morning western civilization class and what squeaky chalk on a blackboard will do to a hangover. In the afternoon they let us loose again on the dirt track. Ol' Richard Howard, who weighs 300 pounds and practically owns the town of Denver, North Carolina, and the Charlotte Motor Speedway, among other things, came over and decided he'd try his hand at the racing. He got in the Impala and I got in one of the Camaros, and we had a pretty good race until I spun out in front of him—twice. He barely missed me both times and I felt kind of stupid, mainly because Buddy Baker and Bud Moore, two of the finest young stock car drivers in the business, had driven up and were watching the action. So I figured as long as everybody else was taking turns in the car, I'd ask Bud if he'd take me around for a few laps and show how it was really done. "Are you kidding? I wouldn't get in one of those damned old cars if you paid me," he said. I thought he was putting me on, because Bud is braver than Dick Tracy and has busted his legs three times racing on dirt tracks against guys like Tiny Lund and LeeRoy Yarbrough.

"No I'm serious man. Those cars are using stock spindles and running gear. Why, if you broke a spindle, you'd flip for sure. And with no roll bars—why, a man would have to be crazy to do that sort of thing," said Bud in the deep, serious voice of his. Just then Garner and Smothers broke over the hill and thundered through the first turn side-by-side, looking like a pair of pros. I looked to Buddy for confirmation. "Bud's right, those damn things are unsafe." Well, then, sports fans, Bud Moore and Buddy Baker had passed judgment just as 37 jillion dollars in entertainment talent went whistling past again, throwing dirt all over hell and acting like Pops and Paul in the good old days. I wondered if Tommy could carry the show alone. Oh well, that was for CBS to worry about.

Garner turned his car over to Snowflake, and that was a mistake. Buddy, Bud, and I were sitting in Buddy's Charger watching ol' Snowflake get progressively farther out of control, and pretty soon Buddy said, "I believe I'll move the car back from the edge of the track. That ol' boy is gonna do something stupid."

Clairvoyance. At that exact moment Snowflake lost it coming down the front straight. He roared past the school's little bus with about six guys inside—missing it by inches—and scattered a mob of guys, including Garner, into a nearby field. Miraculously, the only damage was a wrecked water bucket (used to cool off the Chivalays), but Snowflake had busted up operations for the day. And for Garner and myself, that was about the end. He left the next morning for California to start a new picture called *Support Your Local Sheriff*, and I had to fly to Philadelphia. Somewhere in there is a message.

Smothers stuck around for a few more days with Larry Truesdale and everybody, and I heard later that they let him loose in a Grand National car and he lapped the big speedway at 138 miles per hour—which isn't bad at all. Pops was happy when I left, Snowflake still had the instructors worried, and the Chivalays and the Goodyears were still getting flogged, but nobody had hit the dynamite yet. For that alone, we've all got to be thankful.

Chapter Eleven

CURTIS TURNER:
TO A FALLEN IDOL

He was a purebred southerner, complete with a soft drawl and the kind of clear-eyed courage that seemed part of the DNA in men raised in the hills and hollows of the Piedmont Plateau.

The following stories were written for *Car and Driver*. The first story was published in May 1966, after my first meeting with Turner. The second was published in January 1971 to memorialize his death in a private plane crash. It was a terrible blow to me, and I attended his funeral in Roanoke, Virginia. In those woolly days, death on the race track was a common occurrence and rushing off to funerals would have consumed much of a given year. But Curtis Turner was special. A one-off, not only in a race car, but away from the track, Curtis had—forgive the cliché—a larger than life quality about him, not only in stature but in manner. A savvy but erratic businessman, he had made and lost several fortunes in the timber business. His love life had been a shambles until he married a sweet, beautiful young girl from Spruce Pine, North Carolina, and began to settle down.

His driving career had been interrupted in the early 1960s, when an ill-fated attempt to organize NASCAR drivers in the Teamsters

Union had led to his banishment by his old friend Bill France. Eventually, France relented and Turner returned to the tracks with a vengeance late in his career.

The stories presented here are out of sequence. The first is the memorial to Turner following his death in October 1970. The second is the broader profile that had been written following our first meeting at the Virginia International Raceway in June 1966. Hopefully, between the two, you will gain a stronger sense of my admiration for one of the towering figures in the history of not only NASCAR but of all motorsports.

Curtis M. Turner, Racing Driver, 46
Star of the Grand Circuit Dies in Plane Crash
January 1971

Punxsutawney, PA, Oct. 5 (UPI)—Curtis M. Turner, an auto racing driver, was killed yesterday in a crash of his private plane in Bell Township near here. He was 46 years old and lived in Roanoke, Va.

Mr. Turner, one of the top drivers on the Grand National Circuit, and a passenger, Clarence Drew King, 51, also of Roanoke, were found dead at the scene of the crash in a mountainous area, the State Police said.

The racing driver, who was flying his twin-engine Aero Commander, was scheduled to compete in a 500-mile race at the Charlotte, NC, Motor Speedway on Sunday.

Oh Christ, Curtis went and did it right into the side of a damned mountain, with the throttles open and the nose of that Commander pointed at the sky. Not that anybody figured Pops would stroke out someday in a seedy Morris chair with his grandchildren bouncing on his knee. Not Pops. But to do it when things looked so good. When he was feeling lean and hard and mean and was about to peel off a few hundred grand on another timber deal. And, worst of all, with Bunny's baby due any day. No, it was a little early, because Pops had a lot left in him. He knew how he wanted to die; but that was more of a joke. He used to say he hoped to get hung for rape when he was 103. But once, in a quiet moment with sweet Carolyn Jean ("Bunny"), the little girl from Spruce Pine, North Carolina, who after all those years of his horsing around, was one of those precious few women that meant something to him, he confessed that if it ever came in an airplane, like he suspected, he hoped his hand would be on the throttles when it happened. At least that much worked out.

Curtis Morton Turner, born in Floyd, Virginia, April 12, 1924, the son of Morton and Minnie Turner, the brother of Darnell, Ruby, and Dove, father of Priscilla, Margaret, Sue, Curtis Ross, and Tyler, husband of Carolyn Jean, was some kind of a man. To his dad and mother, he was the embodiment of hill-country machismo—fearless, independent, quick-witted, and committed to the stark ethics that demand a man to be given the household's last scrap of food if he needs it—and that he be killed without remorse if he steals it. To his children he was a fleeting, elusive image who seemed more a charming, itinerant uncle than a father, a man who moved in and out of their lives in the vanguard of the noisy crowds that periodically spread through the big house overlooking Roanoke—bringing them excitement and stimulation but seldom the kind of intense fatherly attention that conventional family life deems necessary.

To his business associates, Curtis Turner was a daredevil speculator; a man who could make and lose hundreds of thousands of dollars in a single day and never find his appetite for financial adventure diminished in the slightest; a man who shielded a robber baron's instinct for business behind a carefully constructed mask of country boy drawls and hesitation; a man who tramped through the fierce, untamed jungle of southern commerce like a hungry lion, picking only victims large enough to fight back and therefore suited to his appetite.

To the millions who watched him drive a racing car, he was the embodiment of heroism. Those who should know say no man who has ever driven a dirt track did so with more skill than Curtis Turner. Others have gone farther, claiming that no one in the history of the sport has ever driven a racing car of any kind better than Curtis Turner. Late in his career, while locked in a struggle with Dan Gurney in the Riverside 500, he negotiated a maneuver that caused Gurney—surely one of the greatest driving technicians—to comment later, "There are probably only two or three drivers in the world who could have done what he did with an automobile. All that they say about him is true."

To the men of the press, Curtis Turner was something of a clown—a zany whose parties afforded them unprecedented opportunities for drinking free liquor and carousing in the swirling circle of friends, associates, sycophants, hangers-on, has-beens, rivals, even outright enemies that seemed towed along behind Turner like debris in the wake of a giant steamship. They stood near him at parties and at race tracks, recording his exploits, writing about the things they felt printable, and using the rest as proof that they were, in fact, integral parts of the Turner world. When he died, only a few of them showed up for the funeral, proving once again the sad fact that most of the greedy, self-serving claque who call themselves journalists realize more than anyone that dead men tell no tales.

As it turns out, they will continue to tell stories about Curtis Turner for generations to come. He was that much an individual— that extraordinary a man. Racing is bulging at the seams with pure nutball characters, men who can drink more, screw more, fight more, laugh more, joke more, than practically any collection of people in the world. It is that kind of a scene, where black humor isn't something Bruce Jay Friedman writes about; it's something you live everyday of your life. In this context, Curtis Turner was a combination of Paul Bunyan, Attila the Hun, and W.C. Fields. You name it, Turner did it—from those famous exploits like landing his Aero Commander on the main street of Easley, South Carolina, on a Sunday morning, to almost single-handedly building the fabulous Charlotte Motor Speedway with some financial acrobatics that would have startled even Big Bill Zeckendorf (an adventure that led to Turner's attempts to organize the NASCAR drivers into the Teamster's Union and his subsequent banishment from Grand National Racing for nearly five years). The Curtis Turner stories are everywhere in the Southland, in and out of automotive circles, and there, from the green ridges of western Virginia all the way down the Piedmont Plateau and into the scrubby flatlands of northern Florida, you can find people—filling station attendants, bankers, bartenders, beauticians, blowsy old broads, and lean, nubile buds of the ilk Turner so fondly referred to as "Baby Dolls," big shots, blowhards, leaders and followers—who will stand you aside and in hushed tones tell you about their encounters with Curtis Turner. It is a raw flax of a great legend that will become part of Southland lore.

No man who ever met Curtis Turner will forget him. I remember my first time with particular pleasure, for no other reason than it led to a friendship, despite our divergent backgrounds.

It was June 1966 at the only Trans-Am sedan race ever run at the Virginia International Raceway at Danville, Virginia. I was supposed to race our Dodge Dart in partnership with David Pearson, except that Pearson managed to blow the engine after four laps of practice and we were out for the weekend. Turner was driving a Mustang with a young New Englander named Pete Lake, and it was the big man's first try at Trans-Am cars. Following the race I had been assigned to write a story on Turner for *Car and Driver* and had asked a long-time friend, Max Muhleman, who before becoming Dan Gurney's manager at All-American Racers, was the best known, most respected southern motorsports writer, to arrange an introduction. Max had known Curtis for many years and had been trying to get us to do a story on him for some time.

A year earlier, David E. Davis Jr., in his annual "In-and-Out Guide" for *Car and Driver*, had informed his readers that "Nothing is more In than getting drunk with Curtis Turner." When Max had informed Turner of this recognition, Pops had asked him, in that deadpan, innocent-kid way of his, "Is that good?"

I approached him in the pits prior to the race, a little reluctantly. I confess that I expected him to be something of a cocky, loud-mouth yahoo, ready to treat a Yankee journalist with about as much conviviality as he would a revenue agent. He was leaning against the side of his Mustang, and he looked even bigger than his substantial 6-foot, 2-inch, 220-pound frame. He was wearing his customary cowboy hat, hung low over his forehead, flush against a pair of Steve Canyon air force sunglasses.

I introduced myself and a hand the size of a tennis racket engulfed mine and a low, drawling voice—soft and friendly—transmitted a greeting. We talked for a while, then Curtis said, "Once this ol' race is done we'll just get in my airplane and fly over to Roanoke and start a brand new party."

Some desperate mechanical ailment befell his Mustang somewhere in the middle of the race, after, if my memory serves me, Curtis looped off the road and felled a pole carrying the race communication phone lines. He packed his driving suit and leading his fiancée, a pretty, rather blank-faced girl named Audrey, and John Griffin, a square-jawed friend who was in the timber business with Turner (or as Curtis would say, "the timberbinnus"), and myself, we marched across the dusty VIR infield to a white Piper Twin Comanche parked beside the back straightaway. Earlier that day Turner had landed his plane on that stretch of roadway, but now it was clogged with buzzing packs of Alfas and Cortinas and thundering clusters of Mustangs and Barracudas.

Over the noise of the racing engines John Griffin said to Turner, "Pops, I believe we'll have to wait for the race to end before we can take off."

Turner regarded a narrow strip of grass separating the track from the spectator fence. "I think we can get off down that li'l strip of grass."

Suddenly I was an interested witness. I had heard of Turner's exploits in the airways and knew that stunts like this were part of everyday life, but the weedy landscape Turner was considering using as a runway rolled away from the airplane for about 50 feet on the level, then plunged into a small dip, rose again to another hump, then fell away to what looked like a drainage gully bordered by a ramshackle fence. From what I could see of our proposed takeoff area, the spot was suitable only for bulldozers, helicopters, and hikers. Nevertheless, we got into the airplane; Turner and Audrey got up front, Griffin and I in the back. Curtis cranked up the engines while John Griffin leaned over to me and whispered, "Curtis is the greatest pilot in the world." I wasn't sure whether he was reporting this fact for his benefit or mine.

The two Lycomings revved up full and Turner released the brakes. The Comanche rolled ahead sluggishly, and then responded with more speed. Loud, thumping sounds came from up from the landing gear as the wheels pounded over the rough earth. Out of the right-side windows I could see the racing cars streaking past. We were going in the opposite direction of their traffic and I can still picture a red Alfa-Romeo GTA that darted suddenly to its left as its driver instinctively jerked away from this winged apparition looming up at trackside. One the left was a collection of spectators leaning against the fence, all of who had glued their eyes on our airplane, in that state of a part-fascination, part-horror experience by those who are about to witness a disaster.

We mounted the second knoll with the engines running flat-out and plunged down into the hollow leading to the gully and the fence. The Comanche wanted to fly, but it simply had not reached the proper simpatico with the laws of physics. It was not going fast enough. Fifty yards left, and Turner was hunched over the controls like a grizzly bear about to dismember a salmon. Then the fence was under us and Turner yanked back on the stick and pulled up the landing gear! We were flying. Six inches off the ground but, by God, we were flying! The Comanche lumbered along in this state of quasi flight for a few moments, then gained enough airspeed to climb out. Turner banked it over in a steep left turn and called back to Griffin, "Hey, Pops, I didn't know whether we was gonna make that 'un or not."

Then he hung the plane on its tail, buzzed the pit area, climbed back out to 4,000 feet and made his famous call for "shooters." Now in case you haven't heard, a "shooter" is a Turner variation on the word "shot," as in "shot of likker," and most particularly refers to a shot of Canadian Club mixed in a few fingers Of "Co-Cola." In a word, a CC and Coke is a shooter, and it was the standard ritual of all Turner flights to lift off, set the aircraft on automatic pilot and have a few shooters.

As I recall, we had about seven shooters before reaching Roanoke. And like the man said, a whole lot of funny people suddenly showed up and a brand new party started.

I don't know what happened to Audrey. She was one of a legion of young ladies Curtis towed around before marrying Bunny. In this particular case he pledged he was going to marry Audrey while driving a stock car around the Charlotte Motor Speedway at 140 miles per hour. "I got us the bravest preacher in the South to say the words," Curtis pledged, but somewhere along the way Audrey and the world's fastest wedding disappeared.

There was something in Curtis Turner that compelled him to dominate his physical environment. He was the ultimate expression of the human factor; a great, good-natured roadblock to the domination of machinery over man—a technocrats' nightmare. Machines—automobiles, airplanes, boats, radios, appliances, you name it—were to be used, not pampered and revered. In this sense there was no greater humanitarian than Curtis Turner. He overwhelmed machines, forcing them to fly, as in the case of the Comanche, when they did not want to fly, or go fast, as in the case of numerous reluctant cars that he horsewhipped to speeds beyond their capabilities. Raw, human will power made things work. It carried him though a million adventures, won him hundreds of races, propelled him places that other men dared not go. He was too big, too independent, too unconventional to be an astronaut, but I swear if he'd been in the program, he'd have made it to the surface of the moon even if he had to drive an Apollo up there like a 10-ton truck.

There was something terribly symbolic about another flight I once made from Atlanta to Charlotte with Curtis in the same Comanche. The night before had involved another massive party and Turner's sleep had been measured in minutes, not hours, before arising for a trip to the Atlanta International Speedway and to qualify for a major Grand National stock car race. We flew from Charlotte early on a muggy, Georgia day and arrived at the speedway after landing the plane at a nearby private strip. Curtis was driving Smokey Yunick's black and gold Chevelle—that same Number 13 that he had put on the pole of the Daytona 500 at a record-breaking 180 miles per hour. It was absurdly simple. Turner arrived at the track, Smokey had the car ready, qualifications began, Curtis climbed into the Chevelle and won the pole position. He removed his giant form through the window of the car and left the speedway. (The same machine, by the way, would send him cartwheeling out of big-time competition at the same track on one of the most spectacular, twisting, turning, rolling, bouncing crashes in the history of the sport. After that, Smokey Yunick refused to field a car for Turner, saying "I don't want to be the man who built the car that killed Curtis Turner." Curtis expressed a different outlook, "Pops, don't think livin' through one of those isn't a great moment.")

Two other men, Richard Howard, the owner of the Charlotte Motor Speedway, and a lawyer whose name escapes me were to fly back to Charlotte with us. The takeoff was typical. No seat belts, no checklists, no engine warm-ups. Just into the cockpit, mag switches on, engines fired up, taxi to the runway, throttles on and into the wild blue yonder. Fly you son-of-a-bitch, fly! We had a couple of shooters, then Turner switched on the automatic pilot and went to sleep. Now this was a common thing on most Turner flights and, in fact, was one of the few chances he had to rest. Often on long trips, he would set the fuel supply on reserve, trusting that the sputtering engines would awake him, permit him to check his position, switch over to the main tanks and steal a bit more rest. Once, high over Winston Salem, North Carolina, on a clear moonless night, I was sitting in the cockpit beside a sleeping Turner and I thought for the first time, "What if we have trouble, or there is a collision or something?" I pondered this for a minute, decided that my ignorance of flying would nullify any chance for me to do anything anyway, and I leaned back and went to sleep too. After that it was easy.

We were about 20 minutes out of Atlanta, Turner was slumbering peacefully, and the lawyer beside me in the rear seat was chain smoking, when I spotted a vast summer storm stretching across the horizon up ahead. Appropriately, we were on a dead aim at the largest thunderhead of the bunch—a malignant-looking giant that was billowing like an H-bomb cloud, at least 50,000 feet into the thick air. For a moment, I thought about warning Curtis, but then was overtaken by a childlike trust that he would awaken at any minute and change course.

He did not.

The initial turbulence n the edge of the storm awoke him, but he did not change course. Obviously regarding the giant thunderhead as some extraordinary challenge of nature, he flew the Comanche into the base of the storm cloud much as a gnat might fly full-bore into the knee of an elephant. Turner was in control now. The automatic pilot was off, his cowboy hat was yanked firmly down over his eyes, and he was locked in personal combat with the storm.

The lawyer had two cigarettes lit. Lightning arced across the sky, and the thunder overwhelmed the sound of the engines. Hail hammered on the windshield and powerful drafts tried to pick the little airplane up and toss it out of the sky. I was overtaken by the absurd serenity—a serenity that can come only when you know that you have lost control of destiny and that you are helpless. John Griffin had once told me that you could tell if you were in trouble with Curtis if he fastened his seat belt. That was the ultimate gesture of alarm. At this moment I could see the chrome buckle of Curtis' belt lying on the cockpit floor. We were going to be all right.

I tried to transmit the bit of obscure intelligence to my friend the lawyer but he was beyond comfort; it was like trying to tell a doomed man that the electric chair won't hurt. He looked at me with eyes in which the pupils were so contracted they were tiny pin holes of fear, and he tried in a palsied fashion to light another cigarette.

Richard Howard finally said it, above the din. "Hey, isn't it kind of dangerous, flying in a storm like this?"

"Ain't too bad," replied Curtis, "Sometimes at night the lightning coming off the wings can hurt your eyes, and 'a course if you don't slow down, the hail might blow out the windshield. Then you gotta fly hunched down behind the instruments panel, and that ain't no fun."

The lawyer, who had been listening to this exchange, slumped back in his seat, positive that he had been abducted by a madman.

Somehow Curtis burrowed his way through the storm and we landed at Charlotte. When he alighted from the plane, the lawyer kneeled down and kissed the macadam runway and wandered away mumbling an oath that he would never fly again.

Other men have had greater adventures with Curtis Turner and they will make sure they are never forgotten. As for me, moments of pure Turner will remain, as in the night of the party at the Mission Inn on the eve of a Riverside 500 stock car race. The big dining room was plugged with race officials, press people, and a multitude of obscure screenland celebs that show up for all the So-Cal races. The other drivers, to a man, had retired, but Pops, as he was known to his friends (not for his parental role, but rather for his old dirt track penchant for "popping" competitors through the fence) was hanging in there with every intention of closing the party and finding himself a baby doll.

The last time I talked to Curtis Turner followed a funny, frantic lunch with Dan Gurney, Max Muhleman, Swede Savage, and AAR's engine expert, John Miller. On the way back to the shop, the subject of Turner somehow entered the conversation, specifically a discussion of his widespread fame as a liquor hauler during his youth and his expertise at bootleg turns. This led Gurney to try a few on the rain-lashed streets of Santa Ana. Muhleman's new Imperial, loaded with four hecklers, hardly simplified Gurney's job, and after narrowly missing a chain link fence and several trees, he managed to lash the monster car around in a mediocre duplication of Turner's famous maneuver—wherein one speeds down the highway, spots trouble (or the fuzz) ahead, punches the brakes and whips the wheel around and ends up roaring away in the opposite direction. Turner was so good at this that I had seen him line a single-lane road with coke bottles and spin a Cadillac Coupe de Ville without knocking a single one over.

Once back at AAR, we called Curtis in Roanoke, where he was impatiently hobbling around on a broken leg received while "horsin' around" at one of his parties. It was a four-way call, with Gurney, Max, and myself on one end, Curtis on the other. We ribbed Dan for a while about what a rotten liquor hauler he'd make, then talked about getting together at a Trans-Am race.

Curtis told Dan they'd have a party that night before the race. Dan knew the routine. He told Curtis that he never drank on the eve of a race. Curtis said, "Hell Dan that's the only way to go racin'. Then you feel so bad you don't give a damn what happens to you." Everybody laughed and said goodbye and Curtis was gone. Then Max said, "You know, Pops wasn't kidding about that business about getting drunk before a race. He actually believes he can drive better with a hangover."

I don't think it was so much that he thought he could drive better hung over; it's just that he thought he could do as well. It was that enormous confidence again, a belief that the Turner mind and body could do anything he willed it to do, including whipping the best race car drivers in the world inside a smoking, fuming race car for 400 miles, 500 miles, even 600 miles. It didn't make no never mind. Curtis knew he could whup you, drunk or sober, in a car or a cocktail lounge, in a plane or peach orchard, on foot or on horseback. He knew he could whup you. And he probably could.

In the end he couldn't keep the Aero Commander in the air anymore. He went into a Pennsylvania hillside, apparently trying to crash land in a nearby strip mine. Another 20 feet of altitude and he might have made it.

They may never figure out what happened, but his friends think they know. Grant Clarence King, the man who died with him, was an old cohort; a golf professional who taught Curtis to play his game. And Curtis attacked golf with a fierce devotion despite an old back injury that prevented him from taking a full swing. In return, Curtis was teaching King to fly. King had a history of heart trouble. Their friends think King had a heart attack and fell into the controls of the Aero Commander. Curtis, faced with the g-forces imposed by the ensuing dive and the bulk of his stricken friend, was unable to clear the controls and could not pull his plane clear of the mountain. Eyewitnesses say that the gear was down and Curtis was struggling to make a landing when the crash came. Thankfully, he was fighting the thing to the very end. For a man like Curtis Turner, that means a great deal.

They buried him in the Blue Ridge Memorial Gardens at the end of the Roanoke Airport in a plot he had picked out. The great men of his sport came to pay homage and to cover his grave with piles of flowers in the form of checkered flags and a special kind of memorial symbolism reserved for southern stock car heroes—a spoked circle of flowers with a segment gone. A broken wheel. Most of the guys who cover stock car racing, while not bothering to attend the funeral, managed to grind out some gigantic reminiscences, tributes, and extended obituaries for their papers. Even *The New York Times*, that smug databank of refined trivia, managed to devote nearly a full column to Curtis Turner. It must have been a mistake, because most of the mannerly, technomen who self-righteously chronicle the course of civilization in the gray pulp log-book, would not have understood Curtis Turner. He was too impulsive, too sentimental, too visceral, too audacious a man to fit their rigid images of worth. By the definitions of *The New York Times*, Curtis Turner was surely not a gentleman. He was, in fact, the kind of beautifully undistilled frontiersmen *Times*men secretly hope will be weeded out of the species, to be replaced by rational, many-sided detached establishmentarians who will lead mankind forward in orderly, measured steps. But such a concept does not take into account the raucous reality of mankind's progress.

Curtis Turner was a passionate man, and *The New York Times*—and in a sense of all of modern humanity—is uncomfortable with passion. Yet there was a little bit of Curtis Turner in all of us, and it seems to me that if civilization's compulsion for order represses the strain that he represented, mankind will have reached its ultimate doom.

Curtis Turner was a helluva man. I hope that wherever he is, he isn't alone.

Who the Hell Do You Think You Are? Curtis Turner?

They call him Pops because he's the roughest, toughest stock car driver who ever lived, and he's popped some ol' boy off the track and through the fence faster than you could wink your eye, I swear. And when Pops ain't manhandlin' some stock car around, chances are he's having himself one of those world famous Curtis Turner parties, with the baby dolls and the hillbilly music and enough of that Canadian Club liquor to keep everybody's motor runnin' 'round the clock. Hot damn! Or maybe he's up in the sky, flying his twin Comanche through thunderstorms and hurricanes, his ol' straw cowboy hat tilted on that mop of black hair, peering through the same ol' sunglasses he wears whenever he steps into the light of day—yep, Curtis Turner is in the air! Maybe on a marathon journey to see some baby doll or maybe on his way to a race or maybe going off to buy himself another 50,000 acres of prime Appalachian timberland. Up there logging more hours on that legend . . .

The phone rings in the pine-paneled office of his sprawling home outside Charlotte and a reedy little voice on the other end drawls, "Ha they'a, is Curtis in?" This is maybe the 11th baby doll to call Pops in the past hour and he comes patiently to the phone, grasping the receiver in a hand that seems large even for his thick-boned, 6-foot, 2-inch frame, "Hey, c-mon over," he says softly, regarding at arm's length a glass of Canadian Club that is lightly diluted with Coca-Cola. "We're gonna start a brand new party in about 10 minutes." He hangs up and smiles. "She ain't a bad li'l ol' baby doll," he announces to John Griffin, a weathered North Carolinian with clear eyes who is Pops' partner in the Carolina Atlantic Timber Company. "I swear," he says, "sometimes I wish I wasn't engaged." Engaged? Curtis Turner engaged? Ain't no way you can keep a man like Curtis Turner tied down by marriage, so what's all this talk about bein' engaged?

"Hey Pops," asked John Griffin, "You ain't really going through with that plan to marry Audrey at Charlotte in a stock car, are you?"

"Hell yes, Pops," says Turner (he called everybody else "Pops," too). "I got me this preacher who says he'll marry me and Audrey while I'm driving a stock car around the Charlotte Motor Speedway at 140 miles an hour. That oughta be the damnedest wedding they ever had in these parts. And that preacher, he's gotta be the bravest preacher I ever did see, I swear."

Audrey Blankenship comes into the room and touches her husband to-be lightly on the shoulder. Audrey is a sweet-eyed 18-year-old from Marion, North Carolina, who is betrothed to this 42-year-old man, who's raised more hell in his lifetime than Frank Sinatra, Shipwreck Kelly, and King Farouk tied together.

"Who was that who just called, Curtis?"

"Ah, nobody, Sweetie, just some li'l ol' girl I used to know. Hey, everybody! Let's get us another tap, we gonna start us a brand new party!"

They go into the enormous bar in the front of the house—a space some innocent architect designed as a dining room. This giant picture window is covered with paintings of frolicking nudes. The room is lit with weird fluorescent "black" light that makes teeth and white shirts glow in the dark and the caricatured baby dolls have these, uh, well, pants, that glow too. Over in the corner is a stereo console, its mahogany top covered with a pile of records. It is blaring an old Rolling Stones number. Domer Reeves and his wife, "Big Red," come in. And here comes Pee Wee, a mechanic buddy of Pops, and a few more ol' boys and baby dolls and pretty soon the room is full. Everybody gets a tap (a "shooter") of C.C. and Coke and all of a sudden, their motors are runnin'! Hot damn! The music gets louder and them ol' boys and the baby dolls are fruggin' away and Curtis gets himself another tap and announces over the din, "Hey, Pops, everything is gonna be all right!" And it is.

Curtis Turner didn't just all of a sudden, one day get to be one of the most famous men in the Southeast. People up around Floyd, Virginia, will tell you Curtis Turner was the best liquor-haulin' driver ever in those parts, and there were a lot of pretty good ol' boys running with Curtis in them days. Curtis Turner was so good he could do a full-speed 180-degree bootleg spin with a 1 1/2-ton pickup on a two-lane bridge and never touch the sides. The police would run him all over the state, but there was no catching him in the McCullough-supercharged, 1940 Ford coupe with the big springs in the back. No way you could catch Curtis, running through the night at 110 miles per hour, up and down through the gears, broadsliding the turns. "Some ol' trooper ran me 39 times," says Curtis, "but he never came close. In those days there was this rule that if they didn't catch you on the road, you were safe, and I used to talk with that ol' trooper and he'd say, 'I'm gonna catch you, if it's the last thing I do Curtis.' Later that ol' boy committed suicide, and some say it was because he could never catch me. I don't know about that, but 39 times sure is a lot."

They caught Curtis once—after he crashed the Ford through the gate of the Little Creek (Virginia) Naval Station with a load of sugar. He had this deal, you see, where he'd take a load of navy sugar into the hills and trade it for white liquor, which he'd in turn sell to the sailors. It was a very satisfying arrangement until certain members of the government heard about it and set a trap for Curtis and his contacts at the base. This one night they let Curtis inside and let him load up with 500 pounds of sugar and tried to arrest him when he came through the gate. But this was Curtis Turner they were trying to stop, and he just crashed through their barricades with the Ford in second gear. They unloaded their .45s and their carbines into the truck, but sugar stops bullets like sand and Curtis fled unharmed into the Norfolk suburbs with a mob of prowl cars and Jeeps in pursuit. By the time he hit the county line and headed down Highway 58 for the hill country, the flashing lights of the law had receded into an otherwise dark horizon. Curtis ran on, free for the moment, but fully aware that every law officer from Norfolk to Charleston, West Virginia, was mobilizing to block his way into the sanctuary of the mountains.

The Ford would burn its pistons after more than 15 miles of full-throttle running on the supercharger, and Curtis motored quietly through a network of short cuts and back roads, trying to conserve his engine and a dwindling gasoline supply. He made it into the foothills of the Blue Ridge Mountains before another patrol car spotted him at an intersection and resumed the chase. Lights exploded in the rear-view mirrors, and the cacophony of engines and tires protesting against the rising speed was punctuated by the dull, wind-lashed reports of pistol fire and the whine of bullets around the cab. Curtis floor-boarded the Ford down a narrow road that crested a series of low hills and managed to open a several-hundred-yard lead on his tormentors.

The author with Curtis Turner at Virginia International Raceway.
Car and Driver archive

The always colorful Curtis Turner ready to race in shirt and tie.
Brock Yates collection

Suddenly the engine faltered. His gas tank was running dry. At that moment the police car dipped out of sight into a hollow and Curtis, still running 100 miles per hour, snapped off his lights and veered into the darkness along the edge of the road. The Ford leaped and bucked through a thicket of scrub pines, finally shuddering to a stop as the lawmen thundered by at full blast. Curtis got out and found himself on the edge of a farmyard, with a school bus parked near his battered Ford. In addition to being out of gas, his lights had been knocked out by the sortie into the underbrush, and Curtis immediately set to work siphoning gas out of the bus and scavenging one of its headlights. This done, he extracted himself from the pines and drove home unmolested . . . smack into the arms of the police, who had the foresight to post a guard around his daddy's place in Floyd.

They carted him back to Norfolk, where he went up before a wise old federal judge who knew a great deal about the business of making and hauling liquor. Curtis explained to him that, what with the war effort and all, there were a bunch of ladies up around Floyd who couldn't make no jelly or bake no pies, and "Well, Your Honor, I was just carrying a little sugar up there to help them ol' gals out." The judge, being as understanding as he was, fined Curtis $1,000 and gave him a two-year suspended sentence.

About that time, Curtis heard that some ol' boys were out racing their liquor-hauling cars every Sunday afternoon in a cornfield near Mt. Airy, North Carolina, and he went down to take a look. The next Sunday he had a go himself. They were a rough bunch of boys, and a lot of metal got bent up in the course of the race, but the cluster of folks who stood on the bank and watched got bigger every week and pretty soon a fellow could make more by racing down at Mt. Airy than he could hauling liquor. Before long, Curtis Turner was racing on other tracks in Virginia and the Carolinas, rubbing fenders with the likes of Fonty Flock, Frank "Rebel" Mundy, Buddy Shuman, Buck

Baker, Marshall Teague, Gober Sosebee, and Red Byron. Very tough boys, they were, but Curtis Tuner could beat them—using a broadsliding, wickedly aggressive style that exploited every last bit of his monumental courage and uncanny coordination.

Led by a tub-thumping, Barnumlike promoter named Bill France, this band of racers in bib-overalls became the biggest sports sensation in the southeastern United States. The National Association of Stock Car Automobile Racing was formed, and the word spread from Tennessee to Florida about how that big ol' boy from Floyd, Virginia, could drive a race car. He raced—and won—at places like Bowman-Gray Stadium in Winston-Salem, North Carolina, where the crowd was so rabid that sometimes he had to beat his way out of the race car with a tire iron, or at Mt. Airy, where he crashed through a board fence twice—once after spinning out and again while reentering the race. And at the nasty half-mile in Charlotte, where he broke his back—the only serious accident he encountered in his two decades of racing. Sometimes he ran for months at a track without being beaten, piling victory upon victory. A southern sports writer recently calculated that Curtis Turner had won 354 feature races, plus an unending string of qualifying heats and minor events. He won so many trophies that the den of his fancy house in Roanoke got plugged to the ceiling. Fed up with the clutter, Curtis began to give them away to friends and casual acquaintances so that now the mantles of hundreds of shoe clerks and insurance brokers who never drove over 65 miles per hour in their lives are sporting giant pieces of silverware awarded for winning contests they would never enter themselves. "Why not?" asks Pops, who may be one of the most generous men alive. "They get a big kick out of 'em and I didn't have any room for them around here. And besides, I sent the best ones down to the Stock Car Racing Museum in Darlington."

By the middle 1950s, Curtis had accumulated a sizable personal fortune in the timber business. Using his vast knowledge of the southern Appalachian timberlands and a bold, but sound, approach to high finance, he rose rapidly in the South's rugged, laissez faire business circles. He remained unchanged through the transition, except for the big house he bought in Roanoke, the better brand of liquor he drank, and the flashier clothes he wore. But money didn't alter the deep hell-country drawl of the grand, uninhibited gregariousness that earned him friends and admirers wherever he traveled. A group of blacks around Richmond are still talking about the day Turner arrived on the scene.

Curtis had just completed a $75,000 timber deal in Richmond and got himself "about tuned" in a postsale celebration. On a whim, he and a few friends drove out to the fairground's dirt track and bought grandstand tickets for the stock car races. Turner had barely settled into his seat when he spotted the black fellows struggling over what appeared to be the poorest car in the whole world. "I believe them boys need some help," said Curtis, leaving his seat in the grandstand. Still wearing a dress shirt and tie, he vaulted the fence and arrived in the pits. Without identifying himself, he made repairs on the exhausted engine, and then climbed into the cockpit and drove the car to a convincing win in the feature. After handing over the winnings to the bewildered but delighted car owners, Turner disappeared into the crowd. It is said that another driver approached them the following week, offering to drive the car, but the owners were firm. "No, sir," they said, "This machine is reserved for the big man in the white shirt and cuff links."

Pops and Joe Weatherly teamed up when the Ford Motor Company got serious in racing in 1955, and they became inseparable buddies. Weatherly was a chunky little Virginian whose good-humored zaniness made him a perfect match for Curtis. It was Joe Weatherly who gave him the nickname "Pops."

Nothing was more fun for either than to give the other's car a clout that would knock it off course during a race. Once, before a

100-miler, Weatherly filled the water bottle in Pop's car with mint juleps and, when Turner was about to take a sip through the rubber tube during a caution flag slow-down, Little Joe pulled up alongside and yelled, "Hey Pops, pass that tube over here and give me a swig."

They rented a house in Daytona Beach together during the annual Speed Weeks and it became the scene of some of the maddest debauches in the Western Hemisphere. They traveled everywhere carousing and chasing baby dolls, laughing and ramming each other off race tracks, until the black day in 1964 when Joe Weatherly died in a crash during the Riverside 500. The combination was broken, and Curtis has not teamed with a driver since.

Joe's death was the culmination of a nightmarish four years that cost Curtis all his money and even worse, a four-year suspension from NASCAR. The source of his troubles was a brilliantly conceived white elephant known as the Charlotte Motor Speedway. It was Curtis' idea from the beginning, and it was his energy and creative talent that were responsible for its design and original financing. It was to have been the best 1 1/2-mile superspeedway in the world, but it was dogged by bad luck from the moment the first shovelful of dirt was turned. To start with, an inaccurate geological survey failed to reveal a massive ridge of Carolina granite that straddled the building site. It took $70,000 worth of dynamite alone to clear that particular obstacle, and there were more problems, both natural and manmade, so its wasn't long before Turner's original $1 million budget had ballooned to $1.9 million. Creditors began to scream, and Pops went through $200,000 of his personal savings in an effort to keep the payments up. He held out for a miraculously long time, managing to reduce the debt to $800,000 before somebody lost patience and went to court.

In a final act of desperation, Turner attempted to float a loan with the Teamsters Union, known for backing long shots. As part of the deal, the Teamsters stipulated that he organize the NASCAR Grand National drivers into the union. This he attempted to do—not out of any commitment to the Teamsters or to the proposition that race drivers should be involved in trade unionism, but only to get the cash for his speedway. He was signing up drivers by the dozens until NASCAR boss Bill France caught wind of the affair and suspended Turner indefinitely. In fact, Pops had every major Grand National star on the roles except, ironically his buddy Joe Weatherly.

The Charlotte Motor Speedway debacle would have broken the spirit of most men. Turner came away from the affair penniless, black-balled from the racing organization that made him famous, and, worst of all, widely accused of stealing hundreds of thousands of dollars out of the track's till. Fortunately, the Justice Department and the Internal Revenue Service spent two years investigating the speedway's tangled ledgers, and in so doing cleared Turner's name.

Pops turned away from racing for a while and devoted his energies to the timber business and amassing another six- or seven-figure bank account. He ran in a few outlaw events around the South—generally on dirt tracks, against second-rate drivers, and his name slowly disappeared form the headlines. Nevertheless, he continued his full-throttle approach to life, complete with the parties that generally staggered on for days at a time. Life was good, and business was booming, but he missed the action and exposure of the major Grand National events. His position as the most famous stock car driver had ostensibly been taken by analytical Fireball Roberts, but the hard-bitten fans hadn't forgotten him.

Turner still remembers an exquisitely reassuring moment on the dark and deserted beach course at Daytona. Pops and John Griffin had been in town on business and, following a few "taps," decided to take their rented car on a couple of laps around the circuit for old time's sake. Daytona racing had long since been transferred to Bill

France's famous Speedway, and the beach track was in a state of ruin by the time Curtis began his nostalgic race through the darkness. He thundered around and around, swinging wide in the sand so the rear wheels rode in the surf, then broad sliding through the neglected banked turns and screeching out onto the macadam back stretch that served as a public road. It wasn't long before one of the neighbors called the cops, and here comes Pops, with a rent-a-car heeled over and its tires folded under, only to find his path blocked by a Volusia County sheriff cruiser. Pops managed to stop in time and sat silently behind the wheel while two deputies approached. A flashlight beam burst in his face and an angry voice yelled. "Who the hell do you think you are? Curtis Turner?"

No, they hadn't forgotten.

The timber business had grown to a point where he had transacted deals on two million acres of land by the time Bill France reinstated him to NASCAR on July 31, 1965. Chrysler was boycotting NASCAR and the all-Ford festival was keeping the crowds home in droves, so France cannily tried to inject some punch into the late-season races by bringing back his biggest name. By then Pops was rich again, what with the timber and the tire franchises and the fleets of trucks and the interests in the shrimp processing plants, but he still wanted to race so bad he could taste it. He accepted France's peace offer instantly.

He'd put on some weight during the layoff and the first few races left him on the edge of collapse. Curtis started in a Petty Enterprises car, crashed in practice, and did not start the race. He next drove for Sam Fletcher at Darlington, then for Rex Lovette twice, and finally hooked up with the Wood Brothers at Martinsville in September 1965. But he refused to reduce his social schedule, telling baffled reporters, "I race better with a little hangover," and he was as likely to arrive at the trace track straight from an all-night party as he was in the halcyon days of the 1950s. Some people said he was too old and too rusty to ever run competitively again, but two months hadn't passed before he won the inaugural American 500 race at the Rockingham, North Carolina, superspeedway. He then added a brilliant drive in the 300-mile Modified stock car race at Daytona. The doubters were silenced. Curtis Tuner was back in force.

He keeps the house in Roanoke exclusively for parties, and nowadays spends most of his time in Charlotte. Regulars in the enormous ranch-style house on Freedom Drive include his three children by a previous marriage and a long-time maid, but the excess beds are generally kept full for a constant flow of old friends who appear unannounced, generally hang around for a few days of partying, and then wander away to nurse their hangovers, catch up on lost sleep, and replenish their precious bodily fluids.

But Curtis rolls on, sleeping two or three hours a night, often restricting his daily food intake to a late-evening sirloin. He has the constitution and physical endurance of a grizzly bear, and countless good men have been reduced to quivering hulks trying to keep pace with his schedule for more than a week at a time. "Hell, if I go to bed without drinking nuthin', I wake up with a hangover, I swear," says Pops solemnly.

So on he goes, getting rich, flying high, driving fast, his motor runnin' flat out. Like he says, "If I was to die tomorrow, I'd be the happiest son of a bitch who ever lived."

And if you've got any sense at all, you'll forget about putting the weed killer on the front lawn and stop worrying about keeping up the car payments and take the next bus, airplane, or train to Charlotte, North Carolina, because Pops says he's going to start a brand new party in about 10 minutes.

Come on boy—git your motor runnin'!

Chapter Twelve

BREAKOUT

While it is now taken for granted that stock racing, NASCAR-Nextel Cup-style, is a monster on television, second only to the National Football League in ratings, there was a day when TV played a relatively minor role in the sport. Races like the Daytona 500 were pretaped and edited, then carried live for the final 90 minutes, always playing second fiddle to such favorites of the day as golf, tennis, and even swimming. Only professional and college football, horse racing, and major league baseball were granted the privilege of full, live coverage, the TV moguls on New York City having little or no interest in understanding a sport they considered to be a redneck, red-clay racing circus at best. In 1971, the Indianapolis 500 was tape-delayed and aired later the same evening on ABC. Races weren't worthy of more coverage according to the geniuses in the faraway skyscrapers of Manhattan.

But by the middle 1970s both ABC and CBS had discovered that automobile racing was resonating in popularity among the American television audience. Coverage increased across the board, with NASCAR, USAC-Indy type racing, sports car competition, and drag racing. But other than Sunday evening coverage by ABC of the Indianapolis 500 and the final 90 minutes of the Daytona 500, the networks chose to deal with the sport in edited, pretaped segments on such shows as *Wide World of Sports* and CBS' *Sports Spectacular.* In most instances, these segments would give way to live coverage of golf tournaments, horse races, and tennis matches, all of which were believed by the moguls to produce higher ratings.

One exception, an executive who believed that motor racing deserved much wider live coverage, was CBS Sports President Barry Frank. He understood that drivers like Richard Petty, Cale Yarborough, and Bobby Allison had gained national stature and that races like those at Daytona, Charlotte, and Atlanta were drawing immense crowds from all over the East Coast. NASCAR Winston Cup racing was billowing out of the Southeast to become a national sport, and Frank believed it was time to exploit its popularity on CBS.

I had been working with the CBS broadcast team covering USAC races and some taped Winston Cup events with announcer Ken Squier. A Vermonter who had risen from his role as public address announcer at the Daytona International Speedway, Ken was to become an expert television commentator and a major advocate of live NASCAR coverage. Working with him was former sports car and Indy car driver, Englishman David Hobbs, who brought his broad knowledge of the sport along with wry British humor to the broadcast booth. I was assigned to pit duty along with Ned Jarrett, the two-time ex-NASCAR champion and a man deeply involved with the inner workings of stock car racing.

After a series of meetings in late 1978 between Big Bill France, his son, and Barry Frank in Daytona Beach, a deal was reached to telecast the 1979 500 live, flag-to-flag. Bill France was a hard man to deal with, in the main because he firmly believed that the key to the success of his sport was a grandstand audience. Television was a powerful adjunct, but not the central reason for its growing popularity. He therefore drove a hard bargain, with the rights fee soaring past

$1.5 million, which included the entire "Speed Weeks" at the track leading up to what Squier would describe on air as "The Great American Race."

I had started with CBS sports on motor racing events at the 1977 Long Beach Grand Prix for Formula One cars and knew the production crew of veteran experts, all of whom had long experience in covering live sporting events. But televising a race that was to last perhaps 4 1/2 hours over a vast landscape presented a new challenge. Twelve cameras were brought to Daytona, eight in stationary positions and four wireless minicams in the pits.

Top driver Benny Parsons, who would later become a fine commentator in his own right, was to carry an early version of an in-car camera. The Australian-designed system would be complex, with the signal from Parson's car transmitted to a helicopter hovering over the track, then sent to a microwave dish at the production truck. A minicam would also be carried on the Goodyear blimp that floated over the speedway during the race.

Mike Pearl was to be the producer, with young Bob Fishman directing. They would head a team of 100 production and administration types who had traveled from New York to set up a field camp for the entire month of February. The affair amounted to a major gamble for CBS and Frank in particular. He had parlayed an enormous load of money and manpower into the project, while his rivals across town in New York at ABC, who had held a comfortable franchise on stock car events, were predicting doom for the entire show.

A week of prerace filming was spent shooting what were called "B-roll" features with Mary Ann Bunce. These were background profiles of drivers and crews that might be inserted into the show in the event of such disasters as a rain-delay, a protracted caution period, or heaven forbid, a hopelessly boring race.

On race day rain showers pelted the northern half of Florida and the producers carried on endless long-distance conversations with New York headquarters as to whether the race would be run at all. This further confirmed doubts within the world of television about the viability of live motor sports broadcasting. Unlike Formula One and sports car competition, American oval track racing was not run in the rain, there being no tires for such situations. If it rained, the Daytona 500 would be postponed until the first dry day. A broadcast on a Monday afternoon, per the contract, would be a ratings disaster and a financial blowout. But if the weather held, it promised to be a great race. A nasty blizzard was pounding the entire northeast, leaving much of the population with little choice but to cozy up in front of their television sets and perhaps watch the first "superspeedway" NASCAR race to be televised from flag-to-flag.

On the morning of February 18, 1979, such familiar faces as Buddy Baker, Cale Yarborough, and the Allison brothers, Bobby and Donnie, were major contenders to face the greatest champion of them all, Richard Petty. Also in the field was a newcomer from Charlotte, North Carolina, whom many touted as a future super star. He was the son of the late, great short-track champion, Ralph Earnhardt. He would be known in later years as the Intimidator, Dale Earnhardt. Also in the field were "rookies" Terry Labonte, Geoff Bodine, and Ricky Rudd—all headed for future stardom.

In those days, the 3,700-pound Winston Cup cars carried stock bodies, compete with grille-work and bumpers. The engines were huge 427-inchers that permitted pole-sitter Buddy Baker and others to rage around the tri-oval at over 195 miles per hour. Speeds at Daytona would continue to escalate for nearly another decade until 1987, when Bill Elliott qualified at the staggering speed of 210 miles per hour. At that point, NASCAR began to impose engine and chassis limits that stabilized speeds, all the while increasing the competition

Cale Yarborough at the wheel of the Wood Brothers No. 21 Ford Torino and on the way to victory in the 1968 Daytona 500. He won by less than a second over LeeRoy Yarborough. *Don Hunter*

Note that Cale Yarborough's 1968 Daytona-winning Ford Torino carries stock grille-work and bumper. While the bodywork was cleverly trimmed to reduce drag, the cars appeared to be essentially stock to the fans in the grandstands. *Car and Driver archive*

and the fender-to-fender racing seen today—despite current lap speeds being almost 30 miles per hour slower than Elliott's peak run.

We arrived at the speedway on race morning to find low clouds blanketing the entire Daytona Beach region. A drizzle spattered the asphalt and the race cars remained inside the open-shed garage area as crews fretted over the possibility that the race would be canceled. Local weathermen scanning the radar in the control tower at the Daytona Beach airport claimed that the low pressure front was moving eastward and the rain would clear by midday. Telephone calls between Mike Pearl and the CBS executives in Manhattan's Black Rock office building remained an open nerve as minute-by-minute decisions were pondered regarding whether the race would be postponed or canceled and what alternate programming would be aired in the four-hour time slot devoted to the race.

As start time approached, the weather began to clear and Bill France and company made the decision that the opening laps would be run under the caution flag to clear any standing water from the speedway.

After the opening ceremonies and the call to start engines, the 41-car field rumbled out. The grandstands were packed and the pits jammed with crews and photographers from around the world. Ned and I split our assignments, with me taking up a position at the far end of the pits near Turn One, where contenders like Donnie Allison, driving Hoss Ellington's car, were located. Ned stood by near the pits of Buddy Baker and Cale Yarborough, who was at the wheel of Junior Johnson's Number 11 car. All would be driving Oldsmobiles, the hottest design of that year. Ironically, for all the NASCAR triumphs recorded by that venerable General Motors brand, it was doomed to be taken off the market within two decades, casting doubt on how much impact race track victories have on real world sales.

It would seem that being stationed in the pits for one of the world's greatest motor races would be an ideal location. But that is hardly the case. Vision is cramped, with only a tiny segment of the track available in the mad clutter of crewman, stacks of tires, and piles of spares. Like Jarrett farther down the pit lane, my only contact with the race was an occasional peek at the leader, Buddy Baker, and the rest of the field loafing behind the pace car; the first 15 laps of the race were run under the caution before it was determined that the track was sufficiently dry for high-speed competition.

Baker got credit for leading the first 15 laps, which were run under yellow. Baker's car faltered at the drop of the green flag and fell back deep in the field, while Donnie Allison bolted into an early lead. Baker was out of the race after 38 laps. Petty, the Allison brothers, Cale Yarborough, and hot Tennessee charger Darrell Waltrip were among the leaders, as were two interlopers, Indianapolis Champion and 1972 Daytona 500 winner A.J. Foyt and the kid from Charlotte, Dale Earnhardt.

While listening to the commentary by Squier and Hobbs as well as signals from the director through my headset, I learned that three of the major players were involved in a mad series of spins on the 31st lap. Coming off the second turn, the Allison brothers and Yarborough looped into the rain-soaked, muddy infield and lost several laps before they were extracted and brought to their respective pits. It appeared that this lash-up early in the race destroyed any chances for these three major contenders.

By midrace, three of the rookies, Earnhardt, Geoff Bodine, and Terry Labonte, were among the leaders, as Baker fell out of contention with mechanical ailments. Meanwhile the mad trio, the Allisons and Yarborough, all in ultrafast machines, were gobbling up the distance and unlapping themselves. A series of crashes brought out the yellow flag, further helping the threesome to catch up. In an amazing combination of great driving and caution laps, the two Oldsmobiles of Donnie Allison and Cale Yarborough were suddenly running nose-to-nose with 20 laps remaining.

I took up station with Hoss Ellington in Donnie's pit, while Ned assumed a similar position with Junior Johnson in Cale's pit.

For lap after lap Donnie and Cale were linked in a nose-to-tail draft. Speeds were unfolding at 193–194 miles per hour as the pair broke away from the pack and headed for a certain last-lap show-down. A.J. Foyt lay third, while Richard Petty was a car-length back in fourth.

In the booth I could hear Ken Squier ratchet up his commentary, correctly predicting that Cale would ride Donnie's bumper until the final corner, then attempt a "slingshot pass" for victory. In those days before the androgynous, slippery body shapes of today, Winston Cup cars could employ a drafting technique that would boost a trailing car around the one in front through a sheer aerodynamic advantage. The only way a lead driver could prevent such a pass was by blocking, which put both cars in jeopardy. With 10 laps to go, I spoke to Hoss Ellington, who with his usual taciturn manner said, "We're gonna have to hold him back if we can." Junior Johnson, equally circumspect, told Ned Jarrett that it would all come down to the final lap. Squier told the massive audience at home that the race would be settled by "one roll of the dice."

I stood by in the Ellington pit, figuring that on lap 200 Donnie would hold off Cale to win or Cale would blow by in a classic slingshot and take the victory. I was wrong. In my headset I heard Squier shouting that on the final lap Donnie and Cale clouted each other on the long, 4,300-foot back straight and, after a few more bunts, both had gyrated into the third turn wall. Pandemonium. Suddenly the checkered flag waved for Richard Petty, who had come out of nowhere to win the 500.

Totally baffled about what had happened, I was sent off to Victory Lane to interview the winner. My headset chattered over what appeared to be a fight on the third turn infield grass between Cale and Donnie and soon to be joined by brother Bobby. I spoke on air with the jubilant Petty, who had just won his sixth 500, admitting that he had resolved himself to a distant third-place finish. In the meantime, I tried to decipher what was going on over on the third turn, where the real drama was unfolding.

I learned later that once the bashed cars of Donnie Allison and Yarborough had juddered to a stop, the pair began a fierce punch-up. Bobby then stopped and entered the fray. Little or no damage was done physically, but the clear loss of a chance to take home the hefty (for those days) $64,000 first place money had triggered the fight.

That battle, plus the intense racing throughout the 500 miles, was a seminal moment for NASCAR. Millions of viewers, many of them isolated by the big blizzard, were exposed to the wild action of big-time stock car racing. The CBS ratings were off the Richter scale, running 10.5 for the whole race and peaking at a record-shattering 13.5 for the final half-hour. There is no question that the 1979 Daytona 500 was a breakout moment for NASCAR, boosting stock car racing, with all its action and suspense, into the consciousness of the American sporting public, where it remains to this day.

But France, despite the monster ratings, was less than pleased with the Allisons and Yarborough. The brawl in front of a national audience upset him and his sponsors, who grumped that such antics belonged in a wrestling match or on a backwater dirt track, but not in the world's most prestigious stock car race. Three weeks later the three combatants were summoned to a hearing involving NASCAR officials in Atlanta prior to the race scheduled there on March 18.

The initial charges were laid against the Allison brothers, who were fined $6,000 each, with the caveat that the fines would be reduced $1,000 for each of the next six races, provided they behaved. In theory the fines were meaningless, but Bobby and Donnie still protested, claiming that Cale was the instigator of the entire affair. The CBS footage of the incident, recorded from several angles, appeared to indict Donnie. He had veered left on the straightaway, apparently blocking Cale as he attempted to pass entering turn three.

But Allison then produced footage shot by a Jacksonville television station from an odd angle that indicted Cale as the one who started the entire affair with his bunt against Donnie's rear bumper. Then came a second impact, also apparently instigated by Cale, although judgment about who was doing what while driving in close quarters at nearly 200 miles per hour in vehicles essentially designed for top speeds half that, remained a moot point. But the NASCAR officials were persuaded that all the blame could not be laid at Donnie Allison's feet and the same $6,000 fine-cum-probation was given to Cale.

But outside the confines of the meeting in Atlanta and the cursory punishments levied against the trio, the impact of the entire race resonated across the nation and particularly in the offices of the major television networks. Barry Frank's gamble paid enormous dividends for CBS and for NASCAR. Overnight, the series became a hot property, with the three giants, CBS, ABC, and NBC recognizing that live NASCAR racing, with all its riveting action and endless drama, was brilliant show business. Within a decade, live Winston Cup was a fixture of weekend sports television, which in turn triggered the massive growth of the stock car racing industry and the steady decline in ratings and sponsorship for the once-revered Indianapolis-type open wheel competition.

Mark the day that Winston Cup racing rose out of the South and spread across the United States as February 18, 1979. With it came a media deluge, with the new Fox network and cable operations like ESPN, the Nashville Network, and Speedvision (now Speed Channel) joining in. NASCAR created its own Motor Racing (Radio) Network (MRN) that broadcasts live coverage of all major NASCAR races into over 300 markets across the nation. Commentators began to chatter about NASCAR from dawn to dark, for the most part shilling the sport with little or no criticism. Television broadcasts were aired with NASCAR'S sanction, so they—like all sporting event coverage—spouted the corporate line, seldom if ever criticizing policy, daring to imply that certain drivers were favored, or that caution flags were tossed to reorder the field. Sponsors were openly promoted, with brand names spouted (The "DuPont Chevrolet," "Home Depot Pontiac," "UPS Ford," "Budweiser Chevrolet," etc.) with such overt pandering that races often became little more than program-length commercials.

Still, the coverage paid big dividends, for the sponsors and manufacturers as well as the networks, who saw NASCAR Winston/Nextel Cup ratings rise to a point where they lay second only to NFL football.

The gamble by Barry Frank in 1979 was long forgotten as live coverage became the order of the day, not only for the big races but for the Busch supporting events, Craftsman trucks, and even qualifying. The nation seemed to have an increasingly ravenous appetite for such programming, and every network, both the majors and the cable operations, jockeyed for more air time. Meanwhile, drivers like Dale Earnhardt Jr. (Little E), Jeff Gordon, Tony Stewart, Dale Jarrett, Rusty Wallace, and newcomers like Ryan Newman, Jimmie Johnson, Matt Kenseth, and Kevin Harvick gathered up their own fan base and became celebrities, as the importance of automobile brands faded into the background.

The old adage, "win on Sunday, sell on Monday," became obsolete as personalities dominated the sport. Pontiac gave up and dropped out, leaving Chevrolet to carry the GM banner, while it became obvious to even the most naive spectator that the NASCAR race cars bore no relationship to those being offered in the showroom. It was accepted that superstars like "Little E" could move from one brand to another without affecting his popularity, much as Richard Petty had proven in the late 1960s when he transferred from his customary Plymouth to Fords.

The power of the personality has long since overwhelmed any true sales potential for selling automobiles, as proven by the sagging market share for the Dodge Intrepid, the Ford Taurus, and the Chevrolet Monte Carlo, all of which in strange, androgynous forms, compete in the Nextel Cup.

The power of the personality is the driving force in the modern world of NASCAR.

Chapter Thirteen

THE TALL MAN IN CONTROL

B ill France Sr. was the craftiest, most creative race promoter in history. His approach to the sport smacked of revolution wherever he laid his handprint. His reasoning about the development of race tracks like Daytona Beach and his masterpiece, Talladega, was elemental: produce an entertaining race and get the people in an out in minimal time. Entrance and egress was his basic mantra and he went to considerable lengths, including the development of major political allies, to achieve his goal.

One such friend was Alabama Governor George Wallace, who produced funding to connect Talladega's front gate with nearby Interstate 20 via a three-mile, four-lane highway. But France's dream track was star-crossed at the beginning.

Slightly longer than Daytona at 2.66 miles and higher banked, the giant place struck fear into the otherwise fearless NASCAR stars. Early tests indicated that it was not only bumpy, but its abrasive surface shredded tires. The Professional Drivers Association (PDA) had been formed in August 1969, and Richard Petty and other stars had already begun to push for better on-track facilities, higher prize money, and reduced speeds. Now came Talladega, with the prospect of even higher velocities and dangerous tire wear. Prior to the first 500-miler, set for September 14, 1969, the PDA announced a boycott.

The drivers walked out late Saturday afternoon on September 13. In an attempt to blunt criticism of his new facility, France borrowed a Holman-Moody Ford stock car and lapped his track at 175 miles per hour, claiming to be the "fastest 59 year-old on earth" and telling the press that if he could race there, surely his superstar drivers could do better. It did not help, and a relative unknown, Richard Brickhouse, won the first Talladega 500 against a thin field. But the race was run without incident, the PDA was shamed out of business, and the union collapsed.

France's political connections paid huge dividends during the OPEC oil embargo that peaked in 1974. With endless gas lines forming across the nation, the Nixon administration established the Federal Energy Office, with the broad goal of decreasing American petroleum consumption by 25 percent.

Cries rose in Congress and in the media to ban automobile racing as a classic example of the profligate waste of gasoline. While Big Bill had ostensibly turned over the presidency of NASCAR to his son, Bill Junior, in 1972, he still held a firm grip on the reins of his organization and took the lead in saving his sport. He quickly announced that NASCAR races would be cut in distance by 10 percent and practice periods would be reduced. France also loudly told the FEO and the press, with the support of his close friend, powerful South Carolina Congressman L. Mendel Rivers, that if motor racing was to be penalized, so should major league baseball and football, which flew charter jets to and from games across the nation. France noted that a Boeing 707, flying coast to coast, consumed more fuel than an entire field of stock cars running 500 miles. This comparison defused further blather in Congress to single out automobile racing.

Big Bill's ardent defense of his sport established him as the visionary able to see racing as a potential rival of the beloved stick and ball games embraced by most of the American public.

He had endured difficult times in the early 1970s, both with the PDA dispute at Talladega and the withdrawal of the factory-backed teams of both Ford and Chrysler. But France countered by signing R.J. Reynolds to a long-term involvement through its Winston brand, and in 1971 the so-called Grand National tour was transformed into the "Winston Cup"—a title it would retain for over 30 years.

He understood that fans came not only to root for various marques ("Ford men" versus "Chevy men," for example) but for individual drivers. Vivid personalities like Glenn "Fireball" Roberts, Richard and Lee Petty, Tim Flock, Marshall Teague, Curtis Turner, Junior Johnson, and other racing legends became enormous box office attractions. They were the essence of southern "good ol' boys' who embodied the public image of wild, ex-bootleggers who had come out of the Piedmont Plateau to bang fenders. This, despite the fact that both Teague and Roberts were Floridians who never hauled liquor, but the imagery enveloped every driver in France's traveling circus. Even northerners like Chicago's Fred Lorenzen and Hoosier Paul Goldsmith, but two of a mass of Yankees who came south to run with the good ol' boys, assumed the roles of simple country boys who could drive the wheels off a race car.

Big Bill knew that fans embraced certain drivers like Fireball and Junior. Popular drivers wining races meant more fans in an escalating business. While pure "hippodroming"—a phrase created in the early part of the twentieth century by touring drivers like the great Barney Oldsfield for fixed races—was never employed, there is little question that rules and caution flags were often jiggered to permit big name stars to win, while newcomers and back-markers played second fiddle.

Bill France used every possible angle to increase the attraction of his sport in the early days, including bloated track lengths, the employment of yellow flags for "debris on the track" to tighten the competition, and giving "the call" to various teams if a special outcome was desired. Competitors understood these realities and were prepared to comply within the growing empire, knowing that in the end "Big Bill" would take care of them. To be sure, there were favorites, determined by those drivers and teams who would attract more fans and therefore increase the gate.

Because his Grand National stockers were inherently slower than Indianapolis-type open-wheelers, he craftily jiggered track lengths to increase lap speeds of what Parnelli Jones and other USAC stars called "taxicabs." This was done simply by altering the length of NASCAR tracks by measuring them differently. Since the early days of horse racing, track distances were measured one foot off the inside rail. But Big Bill revised the system, computing the distance on his NASCAR Speedways one foot off the outside rail. This added extra distance to the track and therefore increased lap speeds. Example: The North Carolina Speedway at Rockingham was originally a one-mile dirt track. When it was revamped into a high-banked oval in 1965 by Darlington developer Harold Brasington, it was still one mile, but in late 1969, NASCAR began remeasuring tracks, and it magically became 1.017 miles, meaning the current 158-mile per hour track record held by Rusty Wallace might be more like 150 miles per hour if the track was measured in the traditional fashion. So too for the incredible Bristol, Tennessee, high-banked "half-mile" that now packs almost 200,000 people into its tiered grandstands that surround the little oval. After opening in 1961, eight years later it amazingly gained a .33-mile extra distance, simply because the length was measured differently. Again, this increased lap speeds, not by quicker automobiles, but by the added distance.

Having earned his spurs in the grass roots of the sport, traveling with his drivers, promoting the races, establishing and enforcing his own rules, and marshalling the funds, Big Bill France became the most knowledgeable and empirical operator in big-time motorsports. He was a phenomenal jack of all trades, a skill that perhaps reached an amusing high point in 1975 prior to the start of the Daytona 500. It was learned that Reverend Hal Marchman, a much respected local preacher, would not be able to give the prerace invocation due to an emergency. There being no other minister immediately available, Big Bill assumed the role. He stepped to the microphone and asked the Lord for good weather, and a safe race. He then paused for a moment, forgetting how to end the prayer. Rather than the traditional "Amen," France stumbled to a conclusion by saying, "Thank you God. Sincerely, Bill France."

For a man sometimes compared to Abe Lincoln, due to his rangy stature and down-home demeanor, this particular public statement would never be compared to the Gettysburg address.

Big Bill never forgot that it was "asses in the seats"—as the old show-biz adage goes—that spelled the difference between success and failure. Filled grandstands were essential, not only to the business, but to the image of the sport. During the early years of the Daytona International Speedway, only the 500 was capable of attracting giant crowds. The July Firecracker 400, the second big event at the track (excluding the modestly successful 24-Hour race for sports cars and a few supporting races for stock cars during the February Speed Week leading up the 500) failed to generate comparable attendance. Rather than reveal to the world that the 400 was not a sellout like the 500, each summer France's crews would take down long rows of temporary grandstands on the outer perimeters of the speedway. In this way no empty seats would be in sight and France could brag that the race was a sellout.

Bill France created an oligarchy that exists to this day, with his son and grand-children. NASCAR was created by a powerful

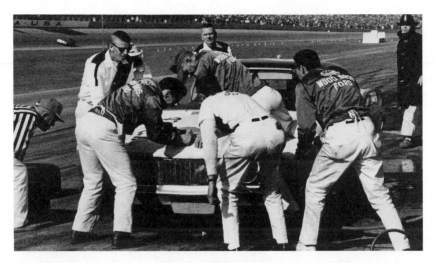

The Wood Brothers crew—among the best in the 1960s—work to reclamp the hood on Cale Yarborough's winning Ford during the 1968 Daytona 500. *Car and Driver archive*

Cale Yarborough and his wife celebrate victory at the 1968 Daytona 500. Note the absence of television cameras in victory lane. *Don Hunter*

dictator and his small, loyal staff of professionals. By contrast, other rival racing organizations like the Sports Car Club of America (SCCA), the United States Auto Club (USAC), and Championship Auto Racing Teams (CART) operated as democracies, with boards of directors and giant committees sluggishly mandating all policies. Meanwhile France and his counterpart in drag racing, the National Hot Rod Association's Wally Parks, and the Indy Racing League's (IRL) boss Tony George, owner of the Indianapolis Motor Speedway, ran their sanctioning bodies with iron hands, depending on their wits, their understanding of the sport and the business, and their personal connections to build NASCAR, the NHRA, and the IRL into successful organizations, while the others failed or remained stagnant. Democracies work well in the world of politics, but Bill France and his family proved conclusively that power in the hands of a few highly dedicated individuals works perfectly in motorsports.

In the beginning, Big Bill envisioned racing in which current models from Detroit battled each other for supremacy. In the late 1940s, over 20 major manufacturers were fighting for market share. Within a decade the field would be winnowed by half, with such major players as Hudson, Studebaker, Packard, Kaiser-Fraser, and Willys disappearing, while the Big Three—General Motors, Ford, and Chrysler—seized command. France's notion of a series that pitted all the major players against each other with their best stock cars was soon altered, and by 1960 NASCAR involved only cars from Ford, Chevrolet, Oldsmobile, Dodge, and Plymouth, with occasional forays by Buick and Mercury. The car models were so-called "hardtop convertible" two-doors, a design that remained in fashion until the middle 1980s. They were well-suited to NASCAR's rules, and for two decades these cars could be transformed into effective race cars while retaining essentially stock bodywork, complete with grilles, bumpers and chrome trim.

But the market was tipped upside down in the early 1970s with the massive invasion of the Japanese. Almost overnight, interlopers like Honda, Toyota, and Datsun (soon to be Nissan) began gobbling up giant shares by the domestic market. The Detroit manufacturers began downsizing, both to compete with the Japanese and to meet the stringent emission regulations that began to be imposed by the Federal government.

Clearly, the old formula would no longer work, in that the giant, 7-liter (427-cubic-inch) V-8 engines were no longer being manufactured, and the two-door hardtop was becoming a thing of the past. Lighter, more efficient four-door sedans, many of which were front-wheel drive, were replacing the old, rear-drive big-engine coupes that formed the core of NASCAR competition.

Moreover, because of more efficient and aerodynamic body designs and improved efficiency from the big engines, speeds were escalating past 200 miles per hour on the superspeedways. France understood that sooner or later one of his cars might vault into the grandstands, which has been fortunately avoided up to that point. Major modifications had to be made in the rules to slow cars down while maintaining the tight fender-to-fender competition that had made the sport so popular.

Long after turning over the leadership to his son, Bill Jr., in 1972, Big Bill remained in control behind the scenes for a number of more years. But time was catching up with him. He had fought the battle to elevate stock car racing into the major leagues—and to displace Indianapolis-style open-wheel racing—for nearly half a century. He had developed strong relationships with the auto industry leaders in Detroit and with powerful political allies in Washington. He had built a massive personal fortune and was also viewed with respect in Europe. His place in the pantheon of motorsports was assured.

But by the end of the 1970s the dreadful hint of Alzheimer's disease began to become evident. He struggled onward, doing his best to guide his son and his strong administration in Daytona Beach, all the while splitting his empire into two divisions: NASCAR, which sanctioned almost 1,500 races across the nation in a variety of minor league series, and the new, publicly traded International Speedway Corporation that owned and operated his centerpiece superspeedways at Daytona Beach and Talladega, plus a network of shorter tracks across the South.

Comforted that he had created one of the greatest sporting empires in history from scratch, William Henry Getty France slowly lapsed into the ravages of his fatal disease and passed away, at age 82, on June 7, 1992. He left behind a legacy that no man before or since could equal.

There is no question that he had his critics. He could be Machiavellian. His goal was simple: create a racing series for stock American automobiles that would be the most entertaining form of motorsport in the nation. The concept of such utopian pursuits as auto racing serving as a fountainhead for technical advances—the refinement of the breed, as it were was secondary to him. The elemental attraction of the masses, who he understood cared not a whit what was under the hood or how the race cars might affect automotive technology, was his goal. Asses in seats. A great show. Such simple goals, well executed, were his mantras. In that context, Big Bill France succeeded far beyond anyone in the history of motorsports and, on a broader scale, perhaps, more than anyone in all of professional sports.

The France family, beginning with its brilliant patriarch; his crafty son, Bill Jr.; and the third generation scions, Brian and Lesa France; live by the same simple theory that motor racing, NASCAR-style, is entertainment, not high-tech rocket science, and that value per dollar for the fans in the seats is the primary mission. Close competition among visible, appealing drivers has produced unbelievable success, with more to come as the sport-cum-show biz expands.

THE CALL

It was for years an unspoken rule in the exclusive realms of the NASCAR garage areas that certain teams would get "the call," i.e., the word from technical inspectors that certain rules would be overlooked for the upcoming race. This might mean larger carburetor jets or plates or more capacity for the fuel call, lighter weight, subtly modified bodywork, or numerous other changes, all of which could easily be accomplished by the master team craftsmen, who could jiggle the specifications like vaudeville magicians. This sort of fiddling was permitted, for example, to increase competition by propelling a slumping but popular driver into contention or to keep a sulking sponsor or manufacturer in play.

Those days are apparently gone, although there are those in within the inner sanctums of the sport who will quietly and privately roll their eyes when speaking about certain victories, like Richard Petty's 200th win at the Daytona Firecracker 400 (witnessed by President Reagan); Jeff Gordon's inaugural Brickyard 400 win in 1994; and the late, great Dale Earnhardt's first and only Daytona 500 triumph in 1998. These and other incredibly popular storybook finishes produced widespread grumping and rumor passing within the NASCAR teams.

Nothing was ever proven, although several top-flight drivers and team owners, speaking in total confidence, maintain that in these three particular races—among many others over the years—the winners got "the call" with machinery that was patently illegal. But intense internecine warfare and open jealousies being at a peak level among the highly charged competitors in NASCAR, such talk could be construed as sour grapes of the worst kind. It is perfectly possible that the Petty, Gordon, and Earnhardt victories were due exclusively to perfect car preparation, excellent pit work, and masterful driving. But many insiders have their doubts.

But there were other occasions when the rules were openly pitched somewhere into the Gulf of Mexico when expediency or internal politics demanded otherwise. In 1981, young Mark Martin rose out of minor league American Speed Association to have a run at the Grand National big time. His car owner was Indiana car builder Ray Dillon, whose chassis were all-winning on the ASA short track circuit. Martin quickly amazed the regulars by winning pole positions at the half-mile Nashville Speedway and at Martinsville shortly after arriving in the Southland. Newcomers were generally not expected to run with the big boys without paying homage to the NASCAR establishment, and at a late-season race, Dillon rolled Martin's car into line for technical inspection.

The NASCAR inspectors, led by the late Dick Beaty and Bill Gazaway, poured over the Dillon machine, pointing out countless violations of the rules—despite the fact that the Hoosier newcomer had scrupulously followed every nuance in the book, understanding that rookies would be subjected to ruthless inspections. But having passed three times before with ease, Dillon felt confident that he faced no problems.

He was wrong. Beaty tore into him, berating him for daring to bring a "cheater" car to the race and summarily heaved him out of the line. Dillon went home. The young man from Indianapolis learned quickly that upstarts never come south and whup up on the local boys without paying a penalty. His driver, Mark Martin, went on to become a NASCAR superstar. Ray Dillon stayed in the ASA.

Chapter Fourteen

RISE TO THE TOP

By the middle 1980s Bill France Jr. was alone at the top, a rather benevolent dictator overseeing a rapidly growing empire that had spread from its southeastern roots across the nation. He had risen out of his father's giant shadow, shucking his early reputation as a rather aimless young man who seemed more interested in pool-playing and partying than assisting his father in the everyday operation of NASCAR and the steady expansion of International Speedway's network of race tracks.

But as Bill France Sr. faded from the scene, Bill Jr. transformed himself into a deadly serious, supremely pragmatic leader of big-time stock car racing. He was facing a radically different set of challenges. His great drivers like Cale Yarborough, Bobby Allison, David Pearson, and his superstar, Richard Petty, were either retired or winding down their careers. Younger men were attempting to take their place, including Georgia's Bill Elliott, Missouri's Rusty Wallace, Texan Terry Labonte, and Tennessee's Darrell Waltrip, as well as a tough, mustachioed kid from Charlotte named Dale Earnhardt.

The son of veteran racer Ralph Earnhardt, who had supported his family through his race track winnings around North Carolina's short tracks, young Dale had stardom written all over him. His father had never ventured far from home to run the Grand National circuit, knowing that his wife and children depended on his weekly purses to put bread on the table. But young Dale, thanks to his dad's training and enthusiasm, left the local racing scene and took a shot at the big time, where he immediately proved he was capable of running with the leaders. After a series of reasonably successful rides with obscure car owners, he linked up with ex-NASCAR driver and team owner Richard Childress and GM's Chevrolet division. He drove a fleet of powerful, excellently prepared Number 3 Monte Carlos, first in yellow and blue Wrangler colors for Childress in 1981 and 1984–1987, then black Goodwrench colors in 1988. His uniquely aggressive and unrelenting style boosted him to seven Winston Cup championships and the pinnacle of fan adoration before his tragic death in the final lap of the 2001 Daytona 500.

If any single driver elevated NASCAR Winston Cup racing to the level of popularity it's enjoyed to this day, the voting would have to be divided between Richard "The King" Petty, and Dale "The Intimidator" Earnhardt.

Working in the background, never seeking the limelight, and content to expand and solidify his father's empire, Bill France Jr., took cautious, pragmatic steps that never smacked of revolution or boat-rocking changes. Surrounding himself with a solid staff of professionals, France moved through the 1980s and 1990s to modify and contemporize the rules that controlled race car design.

The day of the once popular hardtop coupes that had formed the basis for NASCAR race cars was over. Four-door sedans, sport utility vehicles, and pickup trucks were dominating the market. Emission regulations and demands for increased fuel economy had ended the day of the enormous 400-plus-ci V-8s that had powered the stockers for three decades. The changing face of car design in Detroit required alteration in the rules, changes that retained the appeal of the sport without bankrupting the teams by making their existing cars obsolete.

NASCAR race cars were (and are) relatively simple devices compared to the exotic, alloy and carbon-fiber, bewinged and ground-effected Formula 1 and Indianapolis machines. To this day they are essentially 1960s designs, employing pushrod engines (as opposed to the overhead camshaft versions now almost universally used in passenger cars), four-barrel carburetors (no fuel injection, now common in contemporary street cars), tubular steel chassis (no unit bodies like most production models), and solid rear axles (as opposed to the commonly employed independent suspensions on most passenger automobiles).

Avoiding the temptation and the urgings of some in Detroit and the motoring press to update and modernize his cars, France and his team stayed the course, keeping the basic elements of his stock cars intact in the name of stability and tight competition. Like his father, he understood that the essence of his business is entertainment produced by close competition. Exotic technology under the hood meant little or nothing to the multitudes in the grandstands and on television. Other than incremental changes (reducing wheelbase from 115 inches to 110 inches, cutting engine displacement from 427 to 355 ci, and reducing weight from 3,800 pounds to 3,500 pounds) the rules for Winston Cup cars remain steady. The only significant change came with the reintroduction of carburetor plates to limit power, and templates to ensure that the cars retained similar body contours. The templates were intended to eliminate cheating through the subtle chopping and trimming of stock bodies to reduce drag and increase down force.

Slowly this policy produced Winston Cup automobiles that were indistinguishable by brand. From a distance Fords looked like Chevys, which looked like Dodges. Four-doors like the Ford Taurus, the Chevrolet Lumina, and the Dodge Intrepid became two-door coupes. Save for decaled grilles and name badges, they were identical from a distance. But as the importance of the various marques diminished, the power and appeal of the men behind the wheel increased. The marketing power of such young men as Earnhardt and his son, Dale Jr. (better known as "Little E"), Hoosiers Jeff Gordon, and Tony Stewart, Arkansas' Mark Martin and North Carolina's Dale Jarrett, became gold mines for all manner of major commercial entities, from Budweiser to DuPont to Home Depot to UPS to Viagra.

Pickup trucks and cars across the nation began to display Dale Earnhardt's Number 3, Gordon's Number 24, Martin's Number 6, and Little E's Number 8 as the popularity of the drivers reached superstar level.

Sadly, there were losses along the way. Stock car racing remained a dangerous sport, despite the fact that speeds had been chopped by nearly 30 miles per hour from their 210-plus miles per hour peak in the mid 1980s. The human body simply could not survive the massive g-force decelerations caused by impact with solid concrete walls. In 1984 rookie Terry Schoonover died in a crash at Atlanta's International Raceway, while six years later that same speedway claimed the life of Bill Elliott's crewman, Mike Ritch, who was hit by another car during a pit stop.

In 1991 52-year-old J.D. McDuffie, a warrior from the early NASCAR days, was killed in a two-car crash, also involving Jimmy Means, during the running of the Watkins Glen, New York, road-race—one of two such nonspeedway contests held each season. (The other is held on the Sears Point circuit north of San Francisco.) The following year, Bobby Allison's young son, Clifford, died when he crashed against the retaining wall at Michigan International Speedway. This tragedy was only part of a nightmarish series of misfortunes to hit the popular Alabama driver after his own career had ended in a violent crash at Pocono in 1988. On July 11, 1993, his other son, the wildly popular and talented Davey Allison, died when

Drafting, Daytona style. It was quickly learned once the Daytona Superspeedway opened that two cars linked together could run faster than two operating independently. Here, two experts, Buddy Baker in the K&K Dodge and Cale Yarborough in the Junior Johnson Chevrolet, demonstrate the tactic in the 1973 500. *Don Hunter*

Young Bud Moore (no relation to the car builder) spins his Dodge during the running of the 1968 Daytona 500 as the previous year's winner, Mario Andretti, squeezes past. *Car and Driver archive*

his helicopter crashed during landing on the infield of the Talladega Speedway. Earlier that same year, defending Winston Cup Champion Alan Kulwicki had been killed with four others when their private plane crashed in the mountains of Tennessee on the way to a race at Bristol.

The following February, during practice for the Daytona 500, well-liked Neil Bonnett, a fine driver and a member of the old "Alabama gang" headed by the Allisons, was killed in a single-car crash. In August of that same year tough, cocky Californian Ernie Irvan, who was rising to the top in NASCAR, crashed at Michigan International Speedway and suffered what was presumed to be fatal head injuries. Somehow the plucky little man fought his way out of a coma and multiple skull fractures to return to racing, capping his comeback with a 1997 victory at the track that nearly killed him. That accomplished, Irvan retired to his North Carolina farm to raise horses.

As the new millennium arrived, Kenny Irwin Jr., a talented rookie, died in a single-car crash at Louden, New Hampshire's 1-mile oval. Less than a year would pass before the worst tragedy in NASCAR history occurred on the final lap of the 2001 Daytona 500. In a moment of supreme irony as his son, Dale Earnhardt Jr., battled the ultimate winner of the race, Michael Waltrip, the fabled Intimidator spun on the banking of the fourth turn with the finish line in sight and banged the wall almost head on. As the giant crowd and millions at home in front of their televisions watched, the black Number 3 caromed off the concrete wall and slid into the infield grass. At first the crash seemed nearly routine. Dozens of other drivers had experienced similar impacts and walked away. But there was no movement inside the battered car. Kenny Schrader, a fellow driver who had also spun in the accident, was the first to the car and frantically motioned for medical help.

It was useless. The most famous and popular driver since Richard Petty was dead, the victim of a skull fracture that was the result of a strange confluence of force vectors that, if they had been a few millimeters off target, might have permitted the great driver to survive with no more than a sore neck.

As the ambulance motored away from the track, a pall hung over the massive crowd. An atmosphere of doom radiated among them, a sixth sense somehow transmitting the news that what appeared to be a routine accident had been lethal.

Dale Earnhardt's death made headlines everywhere, even in faraway towns hundreds of miles from the nearest race track. The irony was compounded by the fact that the two young men who were contesting for the victory—Michael Waltrip and Dale Jr., were teammates, both at the wheel of cars entered by Earnhardt's thriving racing operation, Dale Earnhardt, Inc., known simply as DEI. As he breathed his last, his son and teammate were inches away from winning one of the most prestigious and important races on the planet.

The inquest was long and exhaustive. Earnhardt's seat belt was examined. The manufacturer, Bill Simpson, a veteran racer and highly respected manufacturer of safety equipment, was initially accused of providing the champion with a defective belt. That theory was discounted, although some claimed that Earnhardt's proclivity for sometimes loosening his belt during long races to aid comfort might have permitted his head to hit the windshield or roll bar, which in turn caused the fatal fracture.

The case dragged on, with the press demanding to see the autopsy photos, which Earnhardt's widow ardently rejected as ghoulish sensationalism.

In the end the accident was written off by most of those close to racing as an act of fate, a tragic moment in a sport that had been nurtured on violence. Men had died at Daytona over the years, although, ironically, none during the running of its most famous race, the fabled 500. Now its greatest active driver was dead, cut down in a freak accident at a point in time when many felt that a modern NASCAR Winston Cup stock car, with its webbing of stout steel protecting the driver, had been refined to a point where it was the safest race car in the world and capable of preserving life in even the most violent crashes.

Any number of great drivers had died at the height of their careers: Bill Vukovich, while leading the 1955 Indianapolis 500, on his way to a third straight victory; World Champions Alberto Ascari, Jimmy Clark, and Aryton Senna; and many others. But somehow the Intimidator seemed larger than life, a rugged, steely man who bordered on immortality.

Stock car fans everywhere mourned his loss, and the Number 3 decal became an omnipresent memorial on automobiles of all sizes and shapes. A statue was erected in Earnhardt's hometown of Kannapolis, North Carolina, and numerous books and articles on his life were published. No man in American automobile racing would be mourned so universally.

Ironically, Dale Earnhardt's death further energized the sport that took his life, elevating television ratings and prompting discussion among segments of the population that heretofore had no interest in stock car racing. This iconic figure, dying in the prime of his life, elicited sympathy—and curiosity—that produced an even greater interest in Winston Cup competition.

NASCAR and its sister property, the publicly held International Speedways Corporation, both under the control of Bill France Jr. and his family, were thriving as the world moved into the second year of the twenty-first century. But there were clouds on the horizon. The leader had survived a long and arduous battle with cancer that had been in part shielded from the public. Treatment for the disease and heart trouble at Jacksonville's Mayo Clinic had nearly taken Bill Jr.'s life, and his struggle back to health had been longer and more difficult than anyone outside the immediate family and his staff had realized.

Back to a semblance of heath, Bill France Jr. realized that it was time to begin the transference of responsibility for running his vast empire to others. Mike Helton, his loyal and capable second in command, would remain in place, but it was imperative that final control lie within the France family, not only to manage the multi-billion-dollar fortune that had been accumulated, but to withstand the threats that lingered outside the perimeter, in the main centered in the booming city of Charlotte, North Carolina, a few hundred miles to the north.

Chapter Fifteen

THE OTHER CENTER OF POWER

I t is presumed that the nexus of power and control of the NASCAR empire lies in the modest building with the checkerboard façade on the edge of the massive Daytona International Speedway. There is the office of Bill France Jr., his son Brian, the heir to the throne, his sister, Lesa, and Bill's brother Jim. From there the France family and its loyal, capable staff control the operations of the NASCAR sanctioning body, plus the events at International Speedway Corporation, which owns four major properties: the superspeedways at Daytona, Michigan International, Talladega, and Phoenix International. Also in the fold are the new Chicagoland Speedway, where a 37.5 percent share is maintained; the Watkins Glen, New York, road course; and the family-owned Martinsville, Virginia, Speedway. Within that group 16 major Nextel Cup races are held annually, while the Motor Racing Radio Network operates in the building, as well as the administration of the thriving Daytona USA amusement park.

There is no question that major policy decisions regarding rules, schedules, and financing of major league stock car racing radiate from that small structure. But to the north, in the Queen City of Charlotte, North Carolina, lies a rival seat of power that remains a restless ally, run by a man with unlimited ambition and the craftiness and acumen to pose a threat to the domination of the France empire. O. Bruton Smith, like Bill France Sr., rose from humble beginnings in the rural South. Growing up in the tiny North Carolina hamlet of Oakboro, Smith entered the retail car business as a young man. As a sideline, he began promoting stock cars races for the newly formed NASCAR series in the early 1950s. Smith teamed with racing star Curtis Turner in the late 1950s to launch the construction of the Charlotte Motor Speedway. This project turned into a star-crossed, underfinanced debacle that ended with Turner and Smith mortal enemies before the first race was organized in the summer of 1960. Following a reorganization of the operation under Chapter 11, Smith hauled it back into the black and by 1975 was the sole owner of the vast property. A daring promoter, he was the first to develop plush VIP suites, adjoining condominium units, a posh restaurant, and enclosed clubhouse seating.

At the same time Bruton Smith was becoming the nation's second-largest car dealer, with over 60 franchises across the South under his control. In the 1990s he began purchasing other NASCAR venues, including the Atlanta International Raceway, the small but prosperous Bristol, Tennessee, half-mile, and the Sears Point, California, road course. In 1995 he took his operation public under the banner of Speedway Motorsports, Inc., which instantly became a hot stock on the New York Exchange. He then purchased the Las Vegas Motor Speedway and in 1997 built the massive 1.5-mile, high-banked Texas Motor Speedway, between Dallas and Fort Worth. This is perhaps the most elegant racetrack in the world.

While Smith had been erecting this massive network of tracks, his home base of Charlotte had become a center of motorsports. The once modestly sized city on the Piedmont Plateau exploded into a world-class financial and trading center, attracting an NFL football team, an NBA basketball club, and an NHL hockey franchise. The Charlotte area also became the home base for most

NASCAR teams. While policy-making remained in Daytona Beach, the geographic location of Charlotte offered obvious advantages to racing operations and their massive support systems.

Good weather most of the year, excluding rare winter ice storms, a confluence of Interstate highways, and a well-educated population made the Charlotte metro area an obvious choice for most of the major racing teams, like those run by Jack Roush, Robert Yates, NFL coach Joe Gibbs, DEI, and others. All these teams built templelike 50,000–100,000-square-foot race shops in the suburbs and in nearby Mooresville. Unlike the early days, when "shade-tree" mechanics built race cars in the yards of their modest homes, these massive operations employed up to 100 engineers, fabricators, engine specialists, mechanics, and office personnel to maintain not one stock car apiece, but fleets of as many as 20 similar machines. Each carried the same livery and to the untrained eye appeared identical. But in the day of specialized racing, individual cars, with different chassis and suspension setups, were built specifically for short tracks like Bristol and Martinsville, road courses like Watkins Glen and Sears Point, 1-mile tracks like Rockingham and Dover, and superspeedways like Daytona and Talladega.

Yet the result of this effort are cars little changed technologically from the Grand National machines of the mid-1960s. All are still fabricated from tubular steel. All still use solid rear axles and independent front suspensions essentially identical to those used 30 years ago, and all are powered by antiquated V-8 pushrod engines, complete with four-barrel carburetors. Yet engine costs have risen to over $50,000 per unit and a top-rank Nextel Cup rolling chassis costs over $200,000. This makes them, in the minds of many, the world's most perfect flintlock rifles.

Annual budgets for these operations, excluding massive support from the Detroit manufacturers with so-called "parts and pieces," is in the $10–20 million range with front-line operations spending considerably more than that. Major sponsorships like those involving Dale Earnhardt Jr.'s Budweiser Chevy, Jeff Gordon's DuPont machine, or Tony Stewart's Home Depot car range between $10–20 million a year, with smaller sponsors paying as much as $2 million for a small decals on the fender or rear spoiler.

The cars are transported to the races, not on open trailers or by tow bars as in the pioneering days, but in million-dollar 18-wheel rigs that serve as rolling machine shops and traveling billboards for the major sponsors.

Not only are the race cars hauled around in style, but the crews travel in luxury, often parking million-dollar Newell and Prevost custom coaches in the race track paddocks. There a staff of chefs and waiters serve drinks and refreshments to crewmen, sponsors, and members of the press during the span of a race weekend. Drivers and car owners in general move from track to track, not in the so-called "Ford motels" of the early years (the back seat of Ford sedans) but aboard their own Lear and Gulfstream private jets.

As the race teams expanded around Charlotte, the impact on area business became significant, not only by the growing employment demands that radiated outward to everything from custom machine shops, foundries, metal suppliers, decal businesses, public relations and marketing firms, but as tourist attractions. The burgeoning fan base, which now rivals that of baseball and football, comes to Charlotte, not only for the races at the great Speedway, but to tour the racing operations, museums, and retail sales outlets. All of this supports a souvenir industry that now exceeds $2 billion annually.

While the power center of NASCAR remains in the hands of the France family in Daytona Beach, the influence and muscle enjoyed by Bruton Smith and his SMI corporation cannot be discounted. Nor can the reality that the two entities are hardly allies,

The Plymouth Superbird arrives. A total of 1,920 of the special, winged machines were built to meet NASCAR's requirement that at least 1,500 models be built for the car to become eligible for competition. Here, Buddy Baker in No. 6 leads the field on a pace lap during a 125-mile qualifying race for the Daytona 500. *Don Hunter*

The war of the super cars. Buddy Baker in his Plymouth Superbird battles Cale Yarborough in his Ford Talladega—a slippery fastback built by Ford to compete with winged Chryslers on Superspeedways. *Don Hunter*

but rather rivals who are siamesed together in a common goal—the expansion and exploitation of the sport of big-time stock car racing.

The fact that almost 80 percent of all Nextel Cup races are held either on ISC or SMI race tracks—including the largest and best attended events that get the highest television ratings—means that a sort of Mexican standoff exists between the two entities. The sport they have created, with powerful inputs from both sides, has ironically transcended both of their influences. It would be impossible for the Nextel Cup to survive if Smith's network of speedways were taken off the schedule. By the same token, SMI would plunge into bankruptcy if its Nextel Cup races were removed from its schedule. Therefore an uneasy truce exists between the two titans, each needing the other to operate. Rumblings of discontent continue, with wild rumors occasionally spreading that Smith is considering the formation of his own stock car league. These are ardently denied, but a lawsuit against NASCAR was initiated by one Francis Ferkel, a surrogate of Smith's, in 2002. The suit claimed that NASCAR was violating antitrust laws in that SMI's Texas Speedway was being denied a second race date, while NASCAR favored its own ISC-owned tracks. The suit was probably frivolous and costly for both sides before it was settled out of court. But there was little or no relief from the tensions that existed between the two giants. A war of billionaires.

Despite these internal wranglings, the two publicly traded stocks do well. The top teams for the most part thrive, although many second-tier operations struggle with rising costs and a lack of sponsorship that is loaded on the more viable operations. The best drivers are millionaires, and now they come from all parts of the nation, as opposed to the early days when they were from the South almost to man.

Charlotte remains the focal point for the major racing operations. The entire area is a hot-bed of racing enthusiasm, and, more importantly, the center of racing commerce. But the locus of influence—the Vatican of the sport, as it were—lies to the south along the east coast of Florida were, almost 70 years ago, an itinerant gas station owner from Washington, D.C., named William Henry Getty France laid down his roots. It remains there to this day.

Epilogue

WHISKEY TRIPPIN' TO THE WALDORF

B y the turn of the century, the France empire had risen to world class levels. The family, headed by the physically frail but mentally tough Bill France Jr., held a dominant position in American motorsports and had become a major business and commercial entity with influence and power that spread across the nation.

The 30-year involvement by Winston, the R.J. Reynolds ciga-rette brand, was about to end. The tobacco giant's infusion of $30 million a year was to be replaced by one of the largest sponsorship deals in the history of all sports, including the Olympics and the National Football League. Nextel, the rising telecommunications company, signed up as title sponsor for $750 million for 10 years—a $75 million payout per annum to have its name on the door of the largest, most lucrative racing series in America. Beyond that, the crafty France Jr., a man once believed to be too distracted by the life of leisure to be a serious successor to his father, had elevated what his dad had started into a monster business. It involved over 2,000 motor races from coast to coast in a variety of national, regional, and local divisions; a network of massive race tracks; a major computer game deal with Electronic Arts; a NASCAR I-Max production; a Daytona Beach motor racing theme park; and no less than 36 supporting sponsors for the Nextel series, ranging from an "official" pizza (Dominos) to an "official" garbage hauler (Waste Management).

The expansion of digital cable systems across the nation had not gone unexploited, and customers could, for $99 a year, receive commercial-free, race-length drivers-eye views from inside six different competing cars. Also available was the opportunity to view all Nextel cup races on a home computer for $66 a year. Fans could simply boot up their PCs and receive constant updates via pit crew to driver radio transmissions and in-car telemetry describing speed and engine performance. If there was any way to connect the fan to the internal workings of the sport, either through network and cable television, theatrical releases, radio broadcasts, or on-line computer links, NASCAR remained aggressively in play.

All major races, excluding the sacrosanct Daytona 500, both in the Nextel Cup and in the Busch Grand National supporting series, also had title sponsors for each event. These included such attractions as the "Cheez it 350" for Busch cars at Bristol, the "Save Mart/Kragen 350" at Sears Points, and the "Albertson's 300 Presented by Pop Secret" at Texas Motor Speedway, proving that there is no apparent limit to the commercialization of big-time stock car racing as run by NASCAR.

Everything at a NASCAR event carries a corporate logo except the lavatory stalls. The cars are plastered with corporate logos, as are the uniforms of the drivers and their crews. More sponsors are waiting in the wings to take advantage of a sport that is now attracting more television viewers than major league baseball, golf, and hockey. Only the National Football League trounces NASCAR in the ratings, as NBC, Fox, and TBS have elbowed each other for rights to the races, knowing that ESPN, Spike, ABC, CBS and others are ready with open checkbooks to cash in on the business. The current television deal brings NASCAR a staggering $2.8 billion until 2008, with a reasonable expectation, presuming a depression, war, or other disaster does not intervene, that the next deal will cost the winning bidders even more.

While the money has become a wallet-busting factor, and the markets have expanded to amazing levels within a network of palatial superspeedways, and the drivers sail around the nation in Lear Jets, the essence of the sport remains exactly the same as that envisioned by Big Bill France and his associates at the Streamline Hotel in 1947.

Their modus operandi was the creation of a series of races in which "stock automobiles" would compete fender to fender and door handle to door handle, piloted by interesting and compelling personalities, who would develop their own fan bases. Much like football and baseball players.

To be sure, their stars were initially ex-bootleggers for the most part, drawn from that talent pool in the Carolinas hills: "good ol' boys" as they referred to themselves. That's exactly how they would be described in the press that slowly became enamored with their raucous life style. That has all changed, with the drivers of today polished and clean-cut athletes who are expected to behave like commercial puppets in public. Only a few—Jimmy Spencer, Kevin Harvick, and Tony Stewart—spill outside the box and behave badly in punch-ups and arguments with other drivers and officials. This inevitably brings massive fines and perfunctory threats of suspension, which seldom happen because NASCAR understands that the bad-boy factor only juices up the show, counterbalancing the choir boys like Jeff Gordon, Dale Jarrett, and Jimmie Johnson, with an occasional rumble from the rabble.

But for all the efforts to create stardom and entertainment value from the drivers, NASCAR remains an essentially all-white, middle-class sport with little or no minority or female participation. There were some female drivers in the early days—Louise Smith, Sara Christian, Ethel Mobley, Ann Chester, Ann Bunselmeyer, and others competed. Christian did quite well, finishing sixth at Langhorne and fifth at Hamburg, New York, the highest finish ever by a female racer in NASCAR Cup competition.

Only five African-Americans are known to have raced in a world that, surely in its pioneer days, was rife with ancient, Dixie-style racism. The most successful black man by far was Virginian Wendell Scott, who struggled through the 1950s and 1960s on meager budgets with second-rate machinery that shielded his considerable talent behind the wheel. He won one Grand National race—the only victory by a nonwhite—on December 1, 1963, at Jax Speedway in Jacksonville, Florida.

Rival Buck Baker, one of NASCAR's ranking stars, was initially declared the winner, but a protest by Scott could not be ignored, in that he was clearly the winner by more than two laps. Scott's feats as the only black driver in an all-white world were immortalized in the 1977 motion picture *Greased Lightning*, starring Richard Pryor.

There were those in the world of NASCAR who understood that by opening up the sport to minorities, a massive new audience was available. Such a visionary was H.A. "Humpy" Wheeler, now the CEO and president of SMI and president of Lowe's Charlotte Motor Speedway. In the mid-1970s Wheeler made a serious effort to attract both women and African-Americans into the business. His first attempt involved Janet Guthrie, an ex-sports car driver and engineer who had been the first woman to race in the Indianapolis 500. In 1976 Wheeler arranged for Guthrie to drive a first-class machine in the World 600 at his Charlotte Motor Speedway. Guthrie drove well, but off the pace, to finish 15th in the long, grueling race. A year later,

A bit of hose artistry as a crewman for A. J. Foyt leaps back over the wall following a tire change at the 1970 Daytona 500. The smallish grandstands in the background have given way to a massive expansion. *Don Hunter*

The essence of NASCAR-style competition: clusters of equally-matched cars running in 180-mile-per-hour packs. *Car and Driver archive*

Wheeler helped promote three women for rides in the Daytona Fire-cracker 400. Guthrie was joined by Europeans Lella Lombardi, who had run some Formula One races, and Christine Beckers, a European sports car driver. All three failed to finish. Guthrie raced again in the September 1977 Labor Day Southern 500 at Darlington, finishing 16th; she never returned to NASCAR, as her racing career was essentially over. Robin McCall, Patty Moise, and Shawna Robinson have competed at the Cup level since Janet.

Following Wendell Scott's retirement in 1973, Wheeler arranged for a test drive by Californian Willy T. Ribbs, a talented black man who had run well in European small formula races and in sports car competition in the United States. Sadly, Ribbs radiated the "black power" attitude in fashion at the time and arrived in Charlotte with what many witnesses describe as a chip on his shoulder. An erratic series of appearances for his test drives, plus a speeding ticket, ended the chances for a young man who clearly had the talent to compete. Ribbs made three more attempts in 1986, at North Wilkesboro, Riverside, and Michigan. He failed to qualify at Charlotte and has never appeared in NASCAR again.

There is no question that an African-American driver could compete in NASCAR, given the opportunity. So too for a woman, but in both cases their overall participation in motor racing of all kinds limits chances to reach the top level. Surely a black or female star would generate both interest and revenue, and there seems little doubt that both groups will appear in the Nextel cup within the near future.

Such a presence would surely fit into the plans for the new leader of NASCAR, 41-year-old Brian France, the son of Bill Jr. and grandson of the fabled founder. He has openly touted his plan to energize the Nextel Cup not as a pure sport or as an automotive proving ground, but rather a powerful entertainment force that will provide stronger competition for the all-powerful National Football

League. NASCAR television ratings remain strong through the spring and summer but sag badly in the face of the NFL autumn lure for the nation's audience. Young Brian has a plan to help his business/sport compete by refining the points race to generate more late-season excitement among the contenders. His idea is to permit only the top 10 drivers in the points standing—and any additional driver within 400 points of the leader in the standings—to compete for the championship in the final 10 races of the season. This has raised hackles among the competitors and the press. Many critics claimed that a driver who had a run of bad luck early in the season, but then found the groove, as it were, by September, would be totally closed out of contention for a high finish. But young France, backed by his father, countered that the dash among the top 10 would serve like the playoffs in professional sports, in which only the best of best are in play at the end.

This break with tradition within months of his taking office amplified the background grumbling that the young man was in over his head, much as had been said about his father 30 years earlier. Moreover, many argued that his adopted sister, Lesa Kennedy France, the president of International Speedway Corporation, is the more astute and qualified of the pair. Her education, packing a degree from elite Duke University, contrasts heavily against Brian's dropout from the backwater University of Central Florida. But despite her respect among the racing fraternity, it is widely agreed that a woman heading the all-male, openly misogynistic world of stock car racing would not be well received in many quarters, especially among the estimated 80 million fans who now follow the sport worldwide.

But regardless of any internal disputes over who runs the operation, the question remains as to whether Brian Zachary France will be able to maintain the expanding power and strength of stock car racing, NASCAR style.

In many ways, he faces the challenge of too much appeal. At this midpoint of the first decade of the new century, NASCAR is top-loaded with sponsors, while Ford, General Motors, and Chrysler, as well as Goodyear Tire and Rubber Company, back the series with millions, not to mention hundreds of sponsors who adorn the flanks of individual race cars.

While it has been traditionally an all-American sport, Toyota now runs in the Craftsman Truck series, with its Tundra pickups powered by special pushrod V-8s required by the rules. They have been specifically designed and built for NASCAR competition. Most agree that the next step for the Japanese company is an assault on the Nextel Cup, which could cause anger and defections from the intensely loyal American fan base. "Buy American" is a powerful force among the followers of NASCAR, and there is uncertainty among insiders as to how they will react if Toyotas begin dominating the Daytona 500 and other major races.

Moreover, if Toyota wins in big-time NASCAR, it is possible that arch-rivals Honda and Nissan will join the fray, both justifying their presence through massive domestic manufacturing operations, which qualify them under the rules that NASCAR cars be "American made." If this were to happen, it would only add pressure to the already escalating costs of NASCAR competition. Race teams are being squeezed by the demand for special cars for each type of race track, and massive staffs of engineers and fabricators. In 2003 the first evidence of out-of-control costs became apparent when the traditional 43-car starting field could not be met at some races without totally noncompetitive cars being permitted to fill the grids. Racing budgets are soaring past $30 million for the contending teams, and superstars like Jeff Gordon and Tony Stewart demand upward of $20 million in salary and promotional deals. The new leader will have to deal with the furious inflation of doing business in NASCAR.

Yet another new wave of future stars is arriving on the scene, most of them defecting from the sagging Indy car leagues. Like current stars Ryan Newman and Kasey Kahne, who in years past would have moved from their sprint car roots into open-wheel Indy cars, young guns like Brendan Gaughan, Brian Vickers, and others might have gone the Indianapolis route. But now, like up-and-coming stars including Scott Riggs, Scott Wimmer, Johnny Sauter, J. J. Yealey, and others, they are hammering on the NASCAR door, seeking top rides in the Nextel Cup. Each day the magnet for drivers, both here and abroad, becomes more powerful and alluring.

The traditional core of appeal of the Nextel Cup remains intact. Races are traditionally decided by a millisecond. Entire seasons are run when all the races are determined by winning margins of less than a total of 10 seconds. When all other so-called major racing events, including the Indianapolis 500 and all Formula 1 contests, offer no more than 10 percent of the starting fields with a realistic chance of winning, that number in a Nextel Cup race expands to 20–25 percent, meaning that crowd appeal and fan loyalty is spread among a large number of drivers potentially capable of reaching Victory Lane. This wide-open competition, in which upset is always a possibility, is but one more reason for the popularity of the sport.

The question for young Brian France and his sister is simple: Can the NASCAR empire be expanded even more? Surely new markets will be exploited, including the thriving Pacific Northwest, where a new speedway is being planned in the state of Washington. Meanwhile promoters of non-NASCAR speedways would sell their first-born into white slavery to gain a date on the schedule, which now encompasses most of the year, with little or no room for expansion.

One major market remains to be exploited—the largest of all, surrounding the New York metro area. For decades, the Frances have understood the need to penetrate Gotham, with only the Pocono track 100 miles to the southwest in Pennsylvania and the Loudon 1-mile speedway 150 miles to the north in New Hampshire currently available. While Pocono lies within 200 miles of a population of 60 million people, it is beyond the immediate New York ADI (Area of Dominant Influence) favored by sponsors, advertisers, and marketers. So too for the Watkins Glen road course 100 miles to the west in upstate New York.

This makes it apparent why rumors have long circulated that a track might be built in the Albany, New York, capitol district, 150 miles north of the New York City, or perhaps Staten Island. Both would be within easy driving distance of Boston and Montreal. It is known that NASCAR fans are more than eager to drive 300 miles to their favorite race tracks, This means that superspeedways situated within this range of New York, Boston, Montreal, Hartford, Buffalo, Rochester, Syracuse, Harrisburg, Ottawa, Toronto, and even Cleveland would strike incredible pay dirt for the France family.

NASCAR already has a presence in the Big Apple with its flashy, diamond-studded annual awards banquet held at the five star Waldorf Astoria. Each season ends with a glittering, black-tie bash that symbolizes the sport's rise from its red-clay roots of a half-century ago. The glamour surrounding this mega-buck affair has elevated it to one of the most prestigious gatherings in the world of major sports, planted as it is in the media and financial center of the world. To some it borders on the pretentious and mildly gauche, but its very presence, its gaudiness, its-over-the-top splendor, serves as a primal scream for recognition in a city hopelessly tardy in realizing that the American heartland embraces a new and vibrant sport with a bright future—perhaps not only in its native land, but around the globe.

INDEX